STRAIGHT FROM THE

Heart

BY LESLEY B. FAY

Simply Beautiful Food from Taos, New Mexico

Dear Pat & Dave
Happy 50th
Wedding Anniversary
Love Lesley
Chef L

Front cover: Lesley B. Fay

Back cover: Taos Tamale Pie *(page 124)*

ISBN 978-0-615-39713-9 53495

Designed and photographed in Taos, New Mexico

Second Printing

Printed in China

This cookbook, written with love,
is dedicated to my mother, Adele Kratka,
who taught me how to cook;
to my father, Miles Kratka,
who taught me about farming; and
to my husband, Peter, whose drive
and support helped me finish this book.

Lesley B. Fay

table of contents

lesley's story

I grew up in the glory days of California, when the fragrance of orange blossoms filled the air and the earth smelled rich whenever the Rain Bird sprinklers irrigated the alfalfa. I can close my eyes anytime I want and smell the memory of our farm in Riverside.

To me, a keen sense of smell is one of the signs of a competent chef: cinnamon and pine remind me of Christmas; fresh-mowed hay, my childhood; Mennen's After Shave, my dad; bourbon and Coke, my grandparents' house in Claremont, California; fresh-baked bread, our family kitchen.

If you really think about it, smell links to taste, to memories, to emotions.

My cooking career was launched at age five in cahoots with Lyn, my twin sister, best friend, cooking buddy, and fellow troublemaker. We made a cake without our mother's help — and without a recipe. The cake didn't bake all the way through, so we took it out of the oven, cut down the dome-shaped top, and put it back in to finish cooking. (I know now, as a pastry chef, that even opening the door when a cake is cooking is risky business.) The cake was chocolate and it passed the test with us so we ate it.

Inspired by our sweet tooth (our mother would not buy sweets for us), we quickly graduated to fudge. On our first try, we reversed the quantities of sugar and salt — an indescribable taste!

I started canning with my mother as soon as I could see the top of the table. We made dill and bread and butter pickles and sauerkraut, and we canned tomatoes, okra, and asparagus. We made jams and jellies of plums, apricots, nectarines, and every berry under the sun.

We grew our own kohlrabi, rutabagas, turnips, potatoes, and popping corn. I grew up eating every vegetable known and loving them all because they were fresh and never overcooked. For

dinner, we'd have fried eggplant as our protein, chilled cucumbers with vinegar and red onions, yellow squash, fresh sliced tomatoes, Swiss chard, and homemade strawberry-rhubarb pie — my dad's favorite. I still love vegetables. Peter, my husband, says he had never eaten as many vegetables in his life as he has since he married me.

Lyn and I were the middle of seven children. My youth was happy and carefree, my wishes as simple as new blue jeans and cowgirl hats. I rode horses, did chores, pulled weeds, and lay on the grass making pictures out of cloud shapes for hours. We rode our bikes through fields, chased each other with snakes, drove tractors, caught mice, and trapped gophers. I dressed like a tomboy and, when I started junior high school, dreamed of being a fluffy girl. (But by then it was too late — fluffy girls are made at age two.) I also knew that my parents did not have enough money to pay the bills, let alone buy girly clothes.

We had a pet raven named Pete, a pig named Petunia, countless dogs and cats, chickens, rabbits, and the occasional guinea pig or rat. The cats and dogs ate Purina kibble out of the same big crock together, next to a matching

Angeles, California. Agua Mansa flourished until January 1862, when a great flood filled the Santa Ana River and destroyed the community. My sister and I rode our horses through this riverbed, and our grandfather used to take us to the Agua Mansa cemetery to read the historical headstones. New Mexico was a part of me before I ever got here, and it seemed later that my life had come full circle — New Mexico had come to Agua Mansa and I had come from Agua Mansa to New Mexico.

I already knew how to cook when I joined 4-H at age nine; but in 4-H, I learned to be a chef. To my relief it was an all-girls group, because even as a tomboy, I was awkward and too insecure to be in a group with boys.

Our 4-H group was all about cooking, sewing, and home décor. All three would become important creative pursuits throughout my life.

Established in the 1920s, when women's work and men's work were delineated more distinctly than today, early 4-H clubs offered practical,

crock filled with water. None of the animals were allowed inside, but the cats and Pete had a system. As soon as we would go upstairs to our room to get ready for bed, Pete would tap on the window with his beak and the cats would meow their "let me in" request, and we would all hang out like we were having a big slumber party.

We lived in Agua Mansa, an historic community and the first non-native settlement in what was then called San Bernardino along the Santa Ana River. This village of settlers from Abiquiú, New Mexico, was one of the largest settlements during the 1840s. Their presence was a buffer against traders and outlaws along the trading route from Santa Fe, New Mexico, to Los

was good and the social life easy. At that time, the restaurant business was plagued with drugs and alcohol—booze and drugs, the great, inevitable career destroyers. It is still an industry associated with substance abuse, but many chefs are turning to sobriety much earlier in their careers.

As a California beach girl of the early 1970s, I entered a time of my life when all I cared about was partying, going to the beach, drinking, and doing drugs. At that time, I was young and it was fun. Everybody I knew was doing it along with me. I never noticed that many of them quit and grew up, and I failed to notice that the lifestyle was starting to destroy everything good about me. As the party started dwindling, and I was spiraling down, people who loved me and tried to help me finally gave up and left. My family confronted me, and I ignored them. I moved states, changed jobs, switched boyfriends, and eventually left the country.

My parents moved to Egypt. They invited me to live with them, hoping a fresh start might give me a grip on my life. I jumped at the opportunity. To this day, my cooking often reflects the influence of Middle Eastern and Mediterranean cuisine. I moved

hands-on home-economics programs to girls, with instruction in canning, cake decorating, meal preparation, and gardening. The focus wasn't just on making cookies or bread, but knowledge of nutrition, the four food groups, and how to prepare a balanced meal. It was the foundation from which I would later build.

I entered my cakes, cookies, and breads in 4-H fairs, from the Indio Date Festival to the Sacramento State Fair, winning awards and ribbons. I loved cooking and it came naturally to me.

I started cooking professionally later in life than most. In my teens and into my twenties, I worked in restaurants, waiting tables, because the money between the island of Cyprus and Cairo, Egypt, trying to settle; but my behavior kept catching up with me. I had an alcoholic boyfriend and, for a while, survived on his income. I eventually had nothing of my own. Something had to happen, but I still could not see my way out.

And then, something did happen and I still can't really explain it. For the first time, I truly saw that the Lesley who was smart, talented, funny, and popular was being held hostage by this alter personality, a sad woman who was full of fear and an ego to cover it all. Stunned to realize what I had become, I turned to friends and loved ones for help. They bolstered my strengths, provided me tough love and helped me grow up at the age of 32.

I stopped drinking and left the boyfriend; I got a great job in Egypt, my own apartment, a car, and most of all, a tremendous amount of self-respect and courage.

I traveled through Europe and India, living for months in cities that interested me. Finally, a friend gently but firmly told me to get on a plane and go home. Wisely, I followed his advice. I moved to San Francisco not knowing anyone, with my few worldly belong-

ings, and tried to start living a normal life again — dating, developing good friendships, and paying my own way. My life became a whirlwind of incredible, joyous opportunity. A couple of years later, in 1988, I met my wonderful husband, Peter. We lived in Mill Valley, married in 1990, and moved to Sonoma, California with our cat, Oxy.

The only thing I had ever loved doing was cooking, but my fear was that if I cooked for a living, I would lose my only joy. I told my fears to a chef friend, and he said, "Lesley, I have never lost my passion."

Along with great encouragement from Peter, that was all I needed to get started on a life-changing experience. I went to the Swiss Hotel and the Eastside Oyster Bar and Grill, both in downtown Sonoma, and worked for free as an intern. I never cleaned more fish or made more raviolis in my life. Even with all that hard work, I knew this was my profession. It didn't take long to discover that I liked pastry work better than anything — partly because it didn't require putting up with the arrogance and remarks of the male line chefs.

I was 36 years old and just beginning my life. I went to work at the Artisan Bakery and started culinary school at the California Culinary Academy on Polk Avenue in San Francisco. I felt like I knew more than anyone in my classes, but I had to earn the credentials. We had to wear chef toques, arrive on time, take tests, and be respectful toward our chefs.
It taught me about protocol and kitchen language. "Mise en place" — everything in its place.

My first job out was at Bistro Don Giovanni, in Napa, owned by Donna and Giovanni Scala. Two of the greatest restaurateurs I know, they also own Scala's in San Francisco. They are my heroes — I learned more from them than from anyone. This couple had worked from the ground up and knew their stuff.

All this time, Peter was traveling as a sales rep for one of the last standing U.S. producers of men's shirts. He was on the road six months out of the year, and it was wearing. We were always looking for ways to get him off the road when, one day, we walked into a little restaurant called Garden Court Café — a Sonoma institution. Prior to that, it was a hangout called Mother Flugger's. It was a tiny space, but we immediately saw its potential.

We offered to buy it, and our offer was accepted. I remember the first day of ownership. Peter had a minor breakdown, and I had to send him home to sleep. He had never worked in a restaurant, and little did either of us know what was in store for us.

We set to work, putting in a new black-and-white tile floor, painting the café a fabulous yellow set off by magnificent flower boxes, and creating adorable accent shelving. We renamed it Fay's Garden Court Café.

It wasn't long before the restaurant became a huge success. It looked like everyone's dream: Sonoma wine country; a cute, quaint restaurant, always busy; and lots of rave reviews from publications like Sunset and the San Francisco Chronicle, as well as from foodies near and far. Folks waited for hours to enjoy our special benedicts, the biggest banana pancakes in the world, or homemade biscuits and jam.

We were too small to have much staff and too busy not to have enough. I was never a morning person, but when you own a breakfast and lunch restaurant, you get up at 4:30 a.m. to get in at 5:00 a.m. to proof the baking and get ready. (I don't think I wore a lick of mascara for the years we owned it — I never had time.)

But once I was up, early morning at the restaurant turned out to be my favorite time. I would have a double or triple espresso and a pecan rum sticky bun, crank up the music, and start baking for the day, with no one to bother me. Sugar and caffeine were my friends. It was the most back-breaking, tiring work I had ever done in my life (except for picking cotton as a kid). We would put out 200 meals in a 42-seat restaurant out of a tiny kitchen. If I stepped off the line for a second, I would lose the timing and drown in tickets. It was so hot in the summer that we would hose ourselves off outside and come back to cook.

I was out to prove how good I was, as I had yet to become the confident cook I am today. So I started packaging my jams and jellies to sell to guests. The products sold well, and since we used them at the restaurant,

I started packing them in both gallons and retail size. After a couple of years, I started bagging my own scone mixes — Lemon Ginger, Cranberry Orange and Sun Dried Tomato and Basil. I expanded the food line to 15 items: dessert sauces, mustards, aioli, preserves, and baking mixes, selling them in my own retail shop and to the top gourmet markets in Northern California.

But the industry was undergoing a radical shift from a small handmade, homemade market to the big business run by grocery buyers that it is today. The big food companies realized they could spin off from the smaller-scale ideas, create a "gourmet product line," and blow out the gourmet food market. Competition was fierce.

We sold the restaurant and decided to start a farm and build a farm stand to sell the Lesley B. Fay food line along with our fresh produce and flowers.

Farming is one of the few indispensable industries and yet it gets so little respect. My father, a graduate of UC Davis, went broke farming. My grandfather had been a truck farmer who sold his produce to small mom-and-pop markets. When chain grocery stores became the norm, mom-and-pop grocers and people like my grandfather were no longer able to make it.

I was so happy that my dad got to see the place and dine frequently at our Sonoma Restaurant. Given the love my dad and I both had for farmers' markets, it was natural to have a road-side stand on the farm. The property was located on Highway 121 between Sonoma and Napa, so we could grow produce, fruit and flowers to sell along with the food line. The area was still a mishmash of neighbors, but we were trendsetters.

We planted 36 fruit trees and 120 regular trees. We put in a large stocked fishpond, copper-accented fencing, an electronic gate — the works. We needed a profit crop; since we were in the Carneros, the ideal place for pinot, we decided to grow pinot grapes. We made a massive investment.

But bad luck was waiting in the wings. The sharpshooter pest that was destroying grapes in all of Temecula was heading our way, and the demise of our

gourmet food business was imminent. In three years, we sold the farm at a minor loss and left Sonoma, bound eventually for Palm Desert, California.

Peter and I bought a small condominium in Palm Desert. We lived a beautiful winter there, playing tennis, walking, going to the gym. We had quasi-retired, and I must tell you, not working is quite divine. When summer began with its 100-plus temperatures, we headed for Taos to find a small place to live, thinking we'd spend summers there and return to Palm Desert in winter. I had loved Taos ever since my sister and I visited friends when they built the Stakeout Restaurant just outside town in 1975. We wondered if we could find a way to live there.

Our lives were sweet and peaceful, but then came the dot-com era that brought robust good fortune followed by precipitous decline. By 2001, we had lost most of our money. Retirement was now a distant dream — we had to find a way to survive. Our Taos plans were scuttled, and we returned to California to make a living. Peter worked for a real estate firm in Palm Desert and I worked as a home interior designer and remodeler.

Design work sparks the same creative, exciting energy as cooking: it's dynamic, pressure driven and highly creative, requiring a keen eye, dexterous hands, and a love of color. Life was good again; we made enough money to return to Taos and begin looking for a second home.

When Peter and I arrived in Taos, the real estate market was in high gear. Peter was busy selling homes, and I was busy with my design business. I was so sure I was never going to cook professionally again that I gave all my cookbooks to the University of New Mexico and actually threw a big box of recipes away! But all the while, I could hear my mother's wise words echoing in my head: "Never say never."

On March 15, 2007, we celebrated the grand opening of Graham's Grille in Taos, New Mexico. It wasn't an auspicious start — we were mired in partner and kitchen problems, and it would be a while before we got our liquor license. In January, I had badly broken my ankle in a skiing accident and was limping around in a clumsy cast. We were facing yet another of the many uphill battles of our lives.

By 2008, Graham's was making a name for itself, its reputation led by its fabulous, unique cuisine, its warm and welcoming ambiance, and its incomparable customer service. Our food is delicious, unpretentious, and affordably priced, so locals and tourists can dine with us often. Our wine list features wines chosen by our expert sommelier to marry with our menu offerings. In 2010 we won the prestigious Wine Spectator award for our wine list.

I cook with love, and Peter greets with affection, and it makes people happy. We thrive on the opportunity to show our appreciation and bring joy to everyone who joins us for breakfast, lunch, or dinner at Graham's.

When my staff finds someone difficult, I ask them to imagine that person as their mother or father and extend the same courtesy. Of course, there will be people who thrive on another's mistakes, but that is the way of things. We might stumble from time to time, but Peter and I will never give up. We will always apologize, do what we can to make it right, and move forward with good spirit into tomorrow. It's been a winning formula so far, and I have no doubt it will carry us through whatever stormy weather we might encounter through the rest of our lives.

The lesson of my life's story is to trust. Even when it was hardest to believe, I was just where I was meant to be: on the way to fulfilling my God-given talents by cooking food with love, working hard (and being grateful that I could), and bringing a measure of kindness and grace to the world.

If I had not grown up on a farm, been poor, had a big family, or been a problem drinker so I could find a sober and satisfying life — or if I hadn't been a twin, married a kind man, or stopped to make a change — none of this might have happened. Everything I have done is a part of who I am. For all of this, for all the people in my life and all the loving teachers along the way, I am deeply grateful.

So, I offer you these recipes *Straight from the Heart* of my life, to the heart of yours. May they bring you joy, peace and satisfaction. May they please your senses and your palate. May they bring fellowship and fun to you and those you love. *Bon appétit!*

acknowledgments

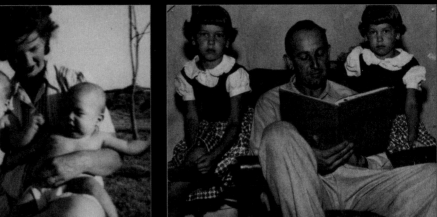

My mother, Adele, taught me how to cook. I know now that my food sense was a God-given gift, but I needed her guidance to direct it. She could create something delicious out of the humblest ingredients—a skill that nurtured her seven children and husband and carried us through the toughest times. I also inherited her sense of humor, her ease with people, and her ability to find solutions to the thorniest problems.

My father, Miles—farmer and man of the earth, who loved dirt—could make anything grow. I loved the smell of wet earth so much that I once tried to eat it. If the grit could be removed, it would be fabulous! My father taught me about farming and fresh vegetables. My weakness for farmers' markets and my love of animals comes directly from him.

My parents raised all seven of their children with a huge garden, immense creativity, and the will to survive a life of unending meals, bills, chores, and squabbles. Their love and influence live on in Straight from the Heart

My heartfelt thanks to my dear friends Neil Stuart and Paula Bernett. Chef Neil, my wonderful mentor, and Paula, poet and writer, helped tell my story and created the title for this book.

appetizers

corn fritters

With Chipotle Honey Butter

3 ears fresh corn

½ cup creamed corn

½ cup green chile, chopped

1 tablespoon butter

3 eggs

1 teaspoon salt

½ teaspoon pepper

¼ teaspoon cumin

½ teaspoon New Mexican red chile powder
(see Resources)

1 pinch oregano

1 cup all-purpose flour, plus extra if needed
(for gluten free, use rice flour)

1 tablespoon cornstarch

1 cup yellow cornmeal or masa harina, plus extra if needed

canola oil for deep-frying

Remove husk and silk from corn. Cut kernels from the cob, measuring 2 cups. Set aside any remaining corn. Crush the 2 cups of corn kernels by pulsing in a food processor. Place in a bowl with the creamed corn, green chiles and any remaining whole-kernel fresh corn.

Melt the butter and add to the corn mixture. Beat the eggs in a clean bowl with the seasonings and pour over the corn mixture.

Add seasonings, flour, cornstarch and cornmeal to the corn mixture. Stir, while adding more of each until mixture has the consistency of a very heavy batter, almost a light dough. It should hold its shape on a spoon but not form a solid ball in your hands. Let the mixture rest in the refrigerator for at least 30 minutes.

When ready to cook, place 2 layers of paper towel on a baking sheet or plate to drain the fritters after frying. Heat the oil in a deep saucepan until it is very hot. Make sure there is enough oil to cover the fritters. Test by dropping a small amount of batter in the oil; it should turn a deep golden brown in about 60 seconds.

Using an ice-cream scoop or spoon, drop one-inch balls of batter in the hot oil, taking care not to splatter. The fritters will turn a deep golden brown in 2 to 3 minutes. If they are browning too quickly or the oil begins to spatter, turn the heat down a little. If they are taking too long, increase the heat.

(continued)

chipotle honey butter

½ can (7-ounce) **chipotle in adobo sauce**
(adjust for heat*)

¾ **pound butter**
(at room temperature)

2 tablespoons water

2 tablespoons tomato paste

¼ **cup fresh cilantro, finely chopped**

1 cup honey

Remove the fritters with a slotted spoon and let them drain on the baking sheet.

Fritters can be held in a warm 275°F oven for up to an hour or refrigerated or frozen for later use. Defrost and reheat in a 350°F oven for 20-25 minutes.

MAKES 30 FRITTERS

CHIPOTLE HONEY BUTTER

Puree chipotle in adobo sauce in a food processor. Add the remaining ingredients and pulse 3-4 times until well combined.

Taste and add extra salt if needed. Refrigerate in a sealed container. This butter is fabulous on cornbread, biscuits and grilled meats.

*Chipotle in adobo sauce varies on heat. If you do not like "hot," add half of the adobo and taste, adding more as desired.

MAKES 2¼ CUPS

duck quesadillas

With Cherry Chipotle Salsa

1 small onion, sliced thin

1 tablespoon butter

1½ cups Monterey Jack cheese, shredded

½ cup Cotija cheese, shredded, plus extra for garnish

¼-½ cup canola oil

8 (6-inch) flour or corn tortillas

1½ cups duck, cooked and pulled off the bones

1 cup Cherry Chipotle Salsa
(see right)

slivered radishes and chopped cilantro for garnish

Melt butter, add onion and cook over low heat until caramelized, about 30 minutes. Onion will be fragrant and a rich golden color.

Put ¼ cup of oil in a large (14-inch) skillet and bring to medium-high heat. Place a tortilla on the bottom of the skillet and add both cheeses, duck and onions. Top with another tortilla.

Let cook until bottom is slightly crispy and cheese begins to melt. Turn quesadilla over using a large spatula. Continue cooking until slightly crispy on the bottom.

Remove from skillet and put on paper towels to drain. Keep warm in a 200°F oven until ready to serve. Repeat with remaining tortillas until all quesadillas are made.

Cut each quesadilla into 4 or 8 sections and garnish with Cotija cheese, slivered radishes and cilantro. Serve with Cherry Chipotle Salsa.

MAKES 4 SERVINGS

This is a great dish to use leftover duck from the Duck Tagine recipe (see page 150).

cherry chipotle salsa

1 tablespoon cornstarch

½ cup sugar

1 cup dried cherries

2 cups cherry juice

1 teaspoon chicken base
(see Resources)

2 tablespoons chipotle in
adobo sauce

2 cloves garlic, minced

2 tablespoons lime juice

1 teaspoon fresh mint, minced

2 tablespoons jalapeños,
seeded and minced

¼ cup fresh cilantro, minced

Mix cornstarch and sugar together. Place cherries, juice, sugar mixture and chicken base in a small saucepan and bring to boil. Simmer for 3-5 minutes. Let cool.

Put remaining ingredients in a food processor and pulse until mixture is chunky, not smooth. Add to the cooled cherry mixture. Serve with Duck Quesadillas.

MAKES 3 CUPS

smoked trout cakes

1 pound smoked trout, flaked

2 cups mashed potatoes

2 eggs

1 cup panko bread crumbs plus extra for coating

1 tablespoon dill, dried

¼ cup capers

2 lemons, zested and juiced

1 teaspoon Old Bay seasoning

canola oil for frying

LEMON AIOLI

2 cups mayonnaise

1 lemon, zested and juiced

½ teaspoon garlic powder

1 tablespoon fresh parsley, minced

¼ teaspoon black pepper

¼ teaspoon salt

¼ teaspoon sugar

pinch cayenne pepper

Put all ingredients except oil, in a large bowl and mix well. I do this with gloved hands. Taste to see if you need to add salt or pepper. The mixture should hold its form when pressed together; if mixture seems too wet, add more panko, if it seems too dry, add another egg.

With a 3-ounce ice-cream scoop, form mixture into cakes. (If you do not have an ice-cream scoop, use a spoon and just make sure the cakes are even in size). Roll each cake in panko and shape with your hands so the tops and bottoms are flat and the sides are rounded, like a hockey puck. Refrigerate until ready to cook, or freeze uncooked for up to one month. Defrost before sautéing.

Cover the bottom of a large skillet with oil. When oil is very hot, lay cakes in the pan. Leave enough room to turn them. When browned, turn over and brown the other side. Remove from pan and place on paper towels to remove any excess oil. The cakes can be left at room temperature for no more than one hour or refrigerated for up to one week. They can be reheated in a 350°F oven for 10-12 minutes before serving. Serve with Lemon Aioli.

Makes 12 to 14 three-ounce cakes

Lemon Aioli
Put all ingredients in a bowl and whisk until smooth.

Makes 2 cups

chicken satay

With Asian Peanut Sauce

2 pounds skinless,
boneless chicken breast

16 (6-inch-long) skewers

SOY GLAZE/MARINADE

½ cup low-sodium
soy sauce

½ cup water

½ cup hoisin sauce

½ cup sake

2 tablespoons
unseasoned
rice vinegar

1 tablespoon
lime juice

2 teaspoons
Thai fish sauce

¼ cup brown sugar

2 tablespoons
cornstarch

2 teaspoons fresh
ginger, peeled
and julienned

1 tablespoon each
minced fresh cilantro,
mint and basil

½ teaspoon
ground star anise
(see Resources)

Cut the chicken into strips ½-inch-wide by 4-inches-long. Place in a large non-reactive bowl or plastic bag and refrigerate.

Prepare the Asian Lime Ginger Soy Glaze by combining all ingredients in a blender, or mix well in a bowl by hand.

Pour marinade over the chicken and refrigerate for at least 2 hours or overnight.

One hour prior to cooking, soak the skewers in water.

Remove chicken from marinade. You can use the marinade as a dipping sauce, by adding an extra ½ cup of water to the mix and bringing it to a boil. Reduce heat and simmer for 20-30 minutes. Otherwise, discard the marinade.

Skewer the chicken and grill over direct medium heat for about 8-10 minutes, turning once or twice to make sure it does not burn.

Serve with the cooked marinade and Asian Peanut Sauce for dipping, along with carrots, peapods and water chestnuts.

MAKES 8 SERVINGS (16 SKEWERS)

asian peanut sauce

¾ cup peanut butter

2 cups coconut milk,
light or full fat

¼ cup lime juice,
freshly squeezed

2 tablespoons
soy sauce

1 tablespoon
Asian fish sauce

1 tablespoon
rice wine vinegar

¼ cup dark brown
sugar packed

1 tablespoon
fresh ginger,
peeled and chopped

4 cloves garlic

2 tablespoons each
fresh mint and cilantro

Put the peanut butter in a blender. Add one cup of coconut milk. Add the remaining ingredients and blend until smooth. Blend in the remaining cup of coconut milk on low speed.

For spicier sauce, add Huyfong Sriracha Sauce, also called rooster sauce, found in the Asian section of most grocery stores *(or see Resources)*. This sauce is also terrific as a salad dressing. Serve as a dipping sauce for the Chicken Satay.

MAKES 3 CUPS

macaroni and cheese

With Green Chile and Smoked Bacon

3 cups dry penne
or elbow pasta

1 cup applewood-
smoked bacon
*(approximately 12 strips,
save two strips for garnish)*

1 cup green chile,
chopped

3 cups Lesley's Famous
Three-Cheese Sauce

SAUCE

1 cup cream

1 cup half and half

⅓ cup sour cream

1 teaspoon
ground cumin

¼ teaspoon salt

¼ teaspoon pepper

3 cups sharp Cheddar
cheese, grated

¾ cup Parmesan, grated

⅓ cup bleu, Roquefort
or Gorgonzola
cheese, crumbled

Cook pasta according to directions and set aside. Best to cook al dente as it will cook more in the cheese sauce.

Fry bacon until crispy and cut into small pieces, reserving some for garnish.

Prepare cheese sauce. Combine all ingredients with cheese sauce. You have several options to cook the Macaroni and Cheese:
1. Cook on the stovetop at medium heat until cheese is hot and bubbly.
2. Microwave on high for 2 to 4 minutes, stirring midway.
3. Cover pan with a lid or foil and bake in a 350°F oven for 12 minutes.

When cooked, divide into four separate ovenproof serving bowls and put under the broiler until the cheese is lightly browned.

MAKES 4 SERVINGS

LESLEY'S FAMOUS THREE-CHEESE SAUCE
Bring cream, half and half, sour cream and spices to a boil. Turn off heat and immediately add the cheeses. Stir well until melted. Do not overcook, as cheese will get stringy. Use right away or cover and refrigerate until needed. Cheese sauce will keep in the refrigerator for up to 3 weeks.

MAKES 3 CUPS

calamari

In Blue Corn Dredge

2 pounds calamari steaks
(place steaks in freezer as they are easier to slice if slightly frozen)

canola oil for deep frying

DREDGE

¾ cup semolina

½ cup panko bread crumbs, ground

2 tablespoons each of ground fennel and star anise

¼ cup sugar

1 tablespoon garlic powder

¼ cup New Mexican red chile powder
(see Resources)

1 tablespoon each ground ginger, dried oregano, ground cumin

¼ cup blue corn flour

1 teaspoon salt

1 teaspoon black pepper

lettuce, fresh lime quarters and blue corn chips for garnish

Finely grind the panko in a blender or food processor. Use a coffee grinder to grind the fennel and star anise.

Mix all dry ingredients together for the dredge and store in an airtight container until ready to use. To bread the calamari, put ½ cup of the dredge on a plate, adding more as needed.

Breading that touches the calamari cannot be reused without risk of contamination. Discard all breading left on the plate.

When ready to fry, heat oil in a deep saucepan until very hot, 350°F. Roll calamari in the dredge and shake off excess.

Place calamari carefully in the hot oil and fry for 1½ minutes, until dark golden brown. They should be tender and not chewy when fully cooked. Remove from pan and drain on paper towels.

To serve, put the calamari on a fresh lettuce leaf with Chipotle Aioli *(see right)*, fresh lime quarters and blue corn chips.

MAKES 8 SERVINGS

chipotle aioli

3 tablespoons chipotle in adobo sauce

2 cups Best Foods or Hellman's mayonnaise

1 teaspoon cumin

1¾ teaspoons lime juice

⅓ teaspoon oregano

2 tablespoons green chile, chopped

pinch black pepper

pinch salt

Puree the chipotle in adobo sauce in a food processor or blender. Combine with the remaining ingredients in a bowl and whisk together until smooth.

MAKES 3 CUPS

oysters nachitos

¾ cup blue-corn flour

¾ cup rice flour

2 tablespoons New Mexican
red chile powder
(see Resources)

canola oil for frying

1 dozen fresh oysters,
shucked

24 blue corn chips

1 cup Pico de Gallo sauce
(see below or use store-bought)

2 avocados, diced

¼ cup Cotija cheese, grated

3 limes, cut into quarters

PICO DE GALLO

2 cups tomatoes,
seeded and diced,
about 4-5 tomatoes
(I like Romas the best)

2 whole jalapeños,
seeded and diced

½ medium red onion,
peeled and diced

2 limes, juiced

2 tablespoons cilantro,
minced fine

pinch each salt, pepper,
ground cumin,
dried oregano

Prepare Pico de Gallo and refrigerate until needed if you are making your own. Mix corn and rice flours together with red chile powder for the dredge and heat oil in either a saucepan or deep skillet on the stove.

Shuck oysters, dip in the flour dredge and fry for about 1 minute until browned. Remove from pan and drain on paper towels.

To serve, lay 2 chips on the plate for every oyster. Place oysters on chips and top with Pico de Gallo, diced avocado, Cotija cheese and a squeeze of lime. If desired, serve with extra lime and Cholula hot sauce.

Makes 12 as an appetizer, 4 as an entrée

Pico de Gallo
Combine all ingredients gently. Let chill and serve.

Makes 2½ cups

chile lime crab cakes

4 cups cooked crabmeat

¼ cup seafood base
(see Resources)

¼ cup lime juice

½ cup corn, uncooked

1 cup red bell pepper,
chopped
(1 large pepper)

1 cup jalapeño chiles,
seeded and chopped fine
(5-6 medium peppers)

1 cup celery, chopped

½ cup cilantro, chopped

1 cup green onions,
sliced thin

½ cup mayonnaise

¼ cup chipotle in adobo sauce

2 eggs, lightly beaten

½ teaspoon each cumin, dry
mustard and black pepper

1 tablespoon each of dried
parsley and dill

1 tablespoon New Mexican
red chile powder
(see Resources)

2 cups panko bread crumbs,
ground, plus 1 cup for dredge

1 cup canola oil for frying

Combine the cooked crabmeat, seafood base and lime juice in a large bowl and mix thoroughly.

Add corn and chopped vegetables to the crabmeat mix. Put the mayonnaise and chipotle in adobo sauce in a blender or food processor and puree.

In a separate bowl, whisk the eggs and stir in seasonings. Add the chipotle mayonnaise and whisk to combine. Pour this mixture over the crabmeat and stir well.

Add 2 cups panko to crabmeat and vegetable mixture. Blend well, adding more crumbs as needed. Crabmeat mixture should roll into a ball easily in your hands without falling apart. It should be firm but not stiff. If it's too dry, add a little more mayonnaise.

For appetizer-sized cakes, form mixture into ping pong–sized balls. Roll the balls in panko then flatten them, forming your hands around the edges to make them straight. They should look like a hockey puck. At this point, the cakes can be refrigerated for up to 7 days or wrapped tightly and frozen for up to 3 months.

(continued)

To cook, heat the canola oil in a sauté pan until very hot. Test by dropping a small piece of bread into the hot oil; it should turn a deep golden brown in 30-60 seconds. After testing the oil, put the cakes in the pan and brown on one side. Turn them over and brown the other side. Remove from pan and place the cakes on paper towels to drain any excess oil.

For burger-sized crab cakes, cook for 6-8 minutes, turning once. If frozen, partially thaw in the refrigerator and increase the cooking time by 2-3 minutes. Serve with Cilantro Red Chile Aioli *(see next page)*.

MAKES 30 CAKES OR 10 BURGERS

cilantro red chile aioli

1½ cups mayonnaise

**1 lime, juiced
and zested**

**2 tablespoons
New Mexican
red chile powder**
(see Resources)

**2 teaspoons
ground cumin**

1 cup fresh cilantro

Put the mayonnaise in a bowl and add the juice and zest from the lime. Whisk in the chile powder and ground cumin. Wash and chop the cilantro and add to the mixture, blending well. Refrigerate until needed. It will keep for 7 days.

MAKES 2 CUPS

muhammara

3½ cups roasted red peppers
(roast your own or use prepared*)

1 small hot Thai
or Serrano chili pepper
*(for more heat, leave in
veins and seeds)*
or 1 tablespoon Turkish
red pepper paste
(see Resources)

½ cup lightly toasted walnuts

½ cup toasted bread crumbs

1 tablespoon lemon juice

2 tablespoons
pomegranate molasses
(see Resources)

½ teaspoon ground cumin

salt to taste

½ teaspoon sugar

2 tablespoons extra virgin
olive oil, more for garnish

**Canned red bell peppers can be
substituted. Drain well, discard stray
seeds and bits of blackened skin.*

This fabulous recipe is wonderfully close to what we would eat in Cyprus. Its origin is Syrian, but it accompanies many Turkish meals. It should be served at room temperature with fresh grilled pita or flatbread.

Roast the peppers and chile over a gas burner or under a broiler, turning frequently until blackened and blistered all over, about 12 minutes. Place in a covered bowl to steam for 10 minutes. Rub off the blackened skins, slit peppers open, and remove stems, membranes and seeds (or leave for more heat). Spread the peppers, smooth side up, on a paper towel and let drain for 10 minutes. Dice the chili pepper and set aside. Toast walnuts in a 350°F oven for about 12 minutes, turning frequently to prevent burning.

In a food processor, grind the walnuts and bread crumbs with the lemon juice, pomegranate molasses, cumin, salt and sugar until smooth. Add the peppers and process until pureed and creamy.

With the machine on, add the olive oil in a thin stream. Add the chile or red pepper paste a little at a time, tasting after each addition. If the paste is too thick, thin with 1 to 2 tablespoons of water. Refrigerate overnight to allow the flavors to merge. To serve, let the dip come to room temperature and sprinkle with extra cumin and drizzle with extra virgin olive oil.

MAKES ABOUT 3½ CUPS

grilled artichokes

With Garlic, Bay, Lemon and Olive Oil

6 medium to large fresh artichokes

3 bay leaves

4 cloves garlic

1 fresh lemon with peel, sliced

½ cup extra virgin olive oil

2 tablespoons kosher salt

vegetable oil for grilling

LEMON AIOLI

2 cups mayonnaise

1 lemon, zested and juiced

½ teaspoon garlic powder

1 tablespoon fresh parsley, minced

¼ teaspoon black pepper

¼ teaspoon salt

¼ teaspoon sugar

pinch cayenne pepper

Prepare the artichokes for grilling by trimming top and bottom and discarding any bruised or damaged leaves. Put into a large enough pot for all to fit comfortably and cover with water. Add remaining ingredients except for extra olive oil.

Cover the pot with foil and place a smaller, heavier pan on top of the foil to weight it down. This will keep the artichokes submerged in the water. Cook for 45 minutes to an hour. They are done when a skewer or toothpick can easily pierce the side of the artichoke. Remove from water and let cool.

Cut the artichokes in half, top to bottom. They will still have the choke (the purple and white area with thistles). Using a melon baller or spoon, scoop out the choke and discard. To grill, preheat the grill to medium. Brush cut sides of artichokes with oil, making sure to coat the heart well. Grill cut side up for 5-10 minutes, then turn over (cut side down) for another 5 minutes. Serve with Lemon Aioli, melted butter or just plain mayonnaise.

MAKES 6 SERVINGS

LEMON AIOLI
Put all ingredients in a bowl and whisk until smooth.

MAKES 2 CUPS

baked lamb ribs

With Chipotle BBQ Sauce

1 onion, peeled

4 cloves garlic

2 celery stalks with leaves

1 carrot, scrubbed

2 pounds lamb ribs
(about 16 ribs)

6 cups beef broth

1½ tablespoons each of
salt and pepper

2 bay leaves

Cut onion, garlic, celery and carrot into chunks. Put ribs in a deep pot and cover with beef broth, adding enough extra water so the ribs are completely covered. Add the chopped vegetables, salt, pepper and bay leaves. Bring to a boil and reduce heat to medium. Cook until ribs are fork tender, about 3 hours.

Remove ribs from water, reserving 2 cups of the liquid for Chipotle BBQ Sauce. Set ribs on a tray to cool. Strain broth and put in the freezer. When the broth has thoroughly chilled, remove layer of fat from the top and prepare Chipotle BBQ Sauce *(see right)*. When ribs have cooled, cut into 2-rib portions per person and trim off excess fat.

To finish cooking the ribs, preheat oven to 300°F and lay the ribs in a large baking dish. Pour on enough sauce to flavor but not cover. Add ½ cup of water. Tightly cover the pan with foil and bake for 30 minutes. Increase oven heat to 350°F, uncover ribs and bake for another 30 minutes, until golden brown. Remove from oven and immediately serve with heated sauce. Ribs can also be cooked, covered, in the oven and then finished on the grill.

MAKES 8 SERVINGS

(continued)

chipotle BBQ sauce

½ cup olive oil

2 cloves garlic

¼ cup each fresh parsley, mint and oregano

¼–½ can chipotle in adobo sauce

¼ cup fresh lemon juice

1 (6-ounce) can tomato paste

½ cup molasses

½ cup packed brown sugar

¼ cup Worcestershire sauce

2 cups lamb broth
(saved from cooking ribs)

salt and pepper to taste

Combine oil, garlic, fresh herbs and chipotle in a blender or food processor and puree. Mix herb blend with remaining ingredients in a large saucepan and bring to a boil. Add salt and pepper to taste. For a sweeter sauce, add more sugar; for a hotter sauce, add more chipotle. For a thinner sauce, add more broth. Cook for 15 to 20 minutes. The sauce and ribs can be refrigerated for up to a week.

MAKES 4 CUPS

rib eye tenders

2 pounds rib eye tenders
(or reasonably tender steak)

20 (6-inch-long)
wooden skewers

2 sourdough baguettes

¾ pound Bleu Cheese Butter
(see below)

MARINADE

½ cup onion, chopped

½ cup oil

½ cup red wine

½ cup red wine vinegar

1½ teaspoons salt

½ teaspoon pepper

2 teaspoons fresh thyme

3½ teaspoons
fresh rosemary

BUTTER

1 pound butter, softened

2 ounces bleu,
Roquefort or Gorgonzola
cheese, crumbled

⅛ cup fresh parsley,
chopped fine

½ teaspoon fresh-
ground black pepper

salt to taste

With Bleu Cheese Butter and Toast

Combine marinade ingredients and put in a non-reactive bowl or plastic bag with the beef and refrigerate for 12-24 hours.

Prepare Bleu Cheese Butter. One hour before grilling, soak the wooden skewers in water.

Remove beef from marinade and cut into ½-inch-wide by 4-inch-long strips. Skewer beef onto sticks and grill for 5-6 minutes over direct medium heat, turning so as not to burn.

MAKES 20 SKEWERS

BLEU CHEESE BUTTER

Mix together all ingredients in a bowl or food processor and chill, covered, until needed.

To serve, bring the butter to room temperature. Slice the baguettes and toast on both sides. Lay the skewered beef on small plates and spread toasted bread with Bleu Cheese Butter.

MAKES ¾ POUND

moroccan bean dip

3 cups cooked hominy

3 cups cooked garbanzo beans

½ cup extra virgin olive oil, divided

1 lime, zested and juiced

2 tablespoons garlic, minced

¼ cup shallots, diced

1 tablespoon cumin

1 tablespoon harissa
(see Resources or page 199)

1 tablespoon ras el hanout*
(see Resources or page 211)

1 tablespoon chipotle in adobo sauce

¼ cup orange marmalade

If using canned hominy and garbanzo beans, rinse thoroughly to remove excess salt. Put half of the hominy and beans along with ¼ cup olive oil in a food processor to blend. When mixture is smooth, transfer to a bowl.

Add the remaining hominy, beans, oil and all other ingredients to the food processor and blend until smooth.

If your processor is big enough, return the first batch to the machine and blend both batches; otherwise mix together in a bowl.

Chill and serve. We serve this dip at the restaurant and it also makes a great vegetarian sandwich filling.

MAKES 7 CUPS

*Ras el hanout is a popular blend of herbs and spices used across North Africa, especially in Morocco. The name means "top of the shop" in Moroccan Arabic and refers to a mixture of the best spices a seller has to offer.

soups

lobster bisque

4 stalks celery

3 shallots or
1 medium white onion

2 medium carrots

1 clove garlic

¼ cup unsalted butter

1 cup each dry sherry
and brandy

12 cups each cream and milk

6 cups water

6 bay leaves

2 tablespoons
Worcestershire sauce

4 cups potatoes, mashed

1 orange, zested and juiced

1 cup lobster base
(see Resources)

1 teaspoon
ground nutmeg

2 tablespoons
Old Bay seasoning

1 tablespoon dried dill

1 teaspoon dried thyme

1 teaspoon pepper

1 tablespoon sugar

½ cup cornstarch

2 cups cooked
lobster meat, chopped

Put celery, shallots, carrots and garlic in a food processor and chop fine. Set aside.

In a large soup pan, melt butter and add chopped vegetables. Sauté until the celery is soft and the onions are clear, about 5 minutes. Add sherry and brandy and cook until alcohol flames.

Add cream, milk, water (reserving ½ cup to make a slurry with cornstarch), bay leaves, Worcestershire sauce, mashed potatoes, orange zest and juice. Stir well and cook over medium heat for 10 minutes.

Mix dry ingredients; seasonings, sugar, and cornstarch. Slowly add ½ cup water, whisking continuously, to make a slurry. Stir cornstarch mixture into cream. Let bisque cook for another 30 minutes at medium heat, stirring regularly.

Remove from heat, let cool for 10 minutes, then pour through a strainer or colander to remove bay leaves and chopped vegetables. If serving right away, put bisque back into pot, adding the cooked lobster and heat through. Garnish with orange zest.

If refrigerating, add the cooked lobster, let bisque cool, pour into a storage container and seal tightly. It will keep, refrigerated, for up to one week.

MAKES 16 SERVINGS

kit carson tortilla soup

1 (14-ounce) can garbanzo beans (chickpeas), drained

1 (14-ounce) can black beans, drained

1 carrot, julienned

1 to 2 cups cooked chicken or turkey, chopped
(turkey was often used, as they hunted wild turkey in Kit's day)

8 cups chicken broth

1 (14-ounce) can diced, cooked tomatoes with juice or 1½ cups diced Roma tomatoes

1½ teaspoons oregano, dried

1 chipotle pepper, chopped

1½ teaspoons ground cumin

1 cup rice, cooked

salt to taste

TOPPINGS

2 avocados

1 cup Monterey Jack cheese, grated

8 each blue or yellow corn tortillas, sliced into ¼- to ½-inch strips

canola oil for frying

Prepare soup by rinsing canned beans thoroughly to remove excess salt. Prepare the carrot and chop the cooked chicken or turkey.

Heat broth to boiling and add chicken or turkey along with beans, vegetables and seasonings. Simmer for 5-10 minutes until the chicken is heated through and carrots are tender. Taste and add more salt if needed. While soup is simmering, prepare the toppings.

To serve, put ⅛ cup of rice in the bottom of each bowl and ladle the soup over it. Garnish with Soup Toppings.

SOUP TOPPINGS

Cut the avocados in half. Remove pit, scoop out the flesh with a spoon and cut into slices. Grate the cheese and cut tortillas into strips.

Heat canola oil in a skillet and fry the tortilla strips until crispy, or put strips on a lightly greased cookie sheet and bake in a 350°F oven for 10 minutes until crisp.

MAKES 8 SERVINGS

chicken and chile posole

**6 cups chicken broth
or 6 cups water
plus ¼ cup chicken base**
(see Resources)

2 cups posole
*(buy it in the freezer section
or use canned hominy,
drained and rinsed)*

1 cup green chile, chopped

**1 cup chicken,
cooked and diced**

**1 teaspoon each of dried
oregano and cumin**

1 small onion, diced

**12-ounce can of
diced tomatoes, drained**

TOPPINGS

**1 cup Monterey Jack
cheese, shredded**

8 flour tortillas, warmed

Put broth or chicken base mixed with water in a large saucepan and bring to a boil. Add remaining ingredients, return to a boil and simmer.

When ready to serve, top with shredded cheese and pass the tortillas. (Warm tortillas, one at a time, in a frying pan for about 30 seconds, turning once. No oil is needed.)

MAKES 8 SERVINGS

watermelon gazpacho

5 cups watermelon,
diced to ¼ inch

½ cucumber, seeded, peeled
and diced to ¼ inch

1 small yellow bell pepper,
seeded and diced to ¼ inch

1 small white onion, peeled
and diced to ¼ inch

3 fresh jalapeño peppers,
seeded and minced

3 cloves garlic, minced

2 cups orange juice

¼ cup fresh lime juice

1 teaspoon each, ground
cumin and dried oregano

1 tablespoon New Mexican
red chile powder
(see Resources)

½ teaspoon allspice

½ teaspoon cinnamon

1 tablespoon each fresh mint
and fresh basil, minced

¼ cup sugar

½ cup red wine
(I like to use sangria)

1 tablespoon extra virgin
olive oil

1 to 2 teaspoons salt

½ teaspoon pepper

Combine all ingredients. Chill for at least one hour. Soup should be served very cold.

MAKES 10 SERVINGS

tomato basil bisque

3 carrots, chopped

3 stalks celery, chopped

1 small onion, diced

3 cloves garlic, minced

1 or 2 tablespoons
extra virgin olive oil

2 cups tomato juice
*(plus ½-1 cup more
if soup seems too thick)*

4 cups diced tomatoes

1 cup fresh basil,
reserve some for garnish

1 tablespoon light
or dark brown sugar

1 teaspoon kosher salt

½ teaspoon fresh
ground pepper

pinch allspice

¼ teaspoon
red-pepper flakes

1 lemon,
zested and juiced

Parmesan cheese
for garnish

Heat oil in a large skillet and sauté the carrots, onion and celery until onions are translucent, then add garlic and continue cooking until garlic is soft. Add tomato juice and cook until vegetables are very tender. Add tomatoes, cover and cook until they are tender. Remove from heat and let cool.

Add remaining ingredients to the soup and puree in a food processor or blender. Pour into a large bowl and adjust for taste by seasoning with salt, pepper or sugar.

Serve hot with fresh minced basil and grated Parmesan cheese; or cold with fresh minced basil.

MAKES 4 TO 6 SERVINGS

ful nabed

With Mint Gremolata

Egyptian Bean and Vegetable Soup

2 cups cooked fava beans or broad beans
(lima, edamame or chickpeas)

1 cup yellow onions, chopped

2 cloves garlic, minced

¼ cup olive oil

2 carrots, chopped

1 teaspoon ground cumin

½ teaspoon ground coriander

2 teaspoons sweet paprika

2 bay leaves

1 cup diced tomatoes, *fresh or canned*

4 cups vegetable stock

¼ cup fresh parsley, minced

1 tablespoon fresh mint, minced

½ teaspoon fresh thyme, minced

1 lemon, zested and juiced

salt and fresh-ground black pepper to taste

Cook fava beans or use canned or frozen beans. If using fresh beans, they must be shelled. In a large pot, sauté onions and garlic in the olive oil until onions are translucent.

Add carrots, cumin, coriander, paprika and bay leaves to the onion mixture and cook over medium heat for 5 minutes. Stir in chopped tomatoes and vegetable stock and simmer until the carrots are tender, about 15 minutes. Add the cooked beans, parsley, mint, thyme, lemon zest and juice. Add salt and pepper to taste. Cook for 30 minutes more over low heat. While the soup is finishing, you can make the gremolata.

MAKES 6 SERVINGS

1 cup fresh mint leaves

½ cup fresh parsley

1 teaspoon lemon zest

1 tablespoon fresh
lemon juice

2 cloves garlic, minced

2 medium pitas, cubed
(about 1 cup)

2 tablespoons
extra virgin olive oil

salt and pepper to taste

MINT GREMOLATA

Combine the first 7 ingredients in a blender or food processor and pulse for 30 seconds to 1 minute or until granular, not smooth. Pulse several times to avoid over-processing. Scrape gremolata into a small bowl and season with salt and pepper. Serve immediately or refrigerate. It will keep for up to one week.

Ladle the soup into bowls and top with gremolata and serve with fresh, hot pita bread.

MAKES 2½ CUPS

green pea and mint soup

¼ cup olive oil

2 shallots, diced

1 clove garlic, minced

2 pounds fresh or thawed frozen peas

½ cup fresh mint, plus extra for garnish

4 cups vegetable or chicken broth

¼ teaspoon nutmeg

1 lemon, zested and juiced

½ cup heavy cream

1 teaspoon kosher salt

½ teaspoon fresh-ground pepper

Unsweetened cream for garnish

Heat olive oil in a large skillet. Sauté the shallots until translucent and then add the garlic, sautéing for 1 minute more. (Garlic cooks faster than onions or shallots so it will burn if you cook them together.) Remove from heat and let cool.

In a food processor, puree the green peas with the mint; add broth in small amounts. With the last batch of broth, add the garlic and shallot sauté, nutmeg and lemon zest and juice. Stir in cream. Adjust for taste with salt, pepper, nutmeg, or sugar.

Serve hot or cold. Garnish each serving with fresh mint and a dollop of unsweetened cream.

MAKES 4 TO 6 SERVINGS

cold andalusian soup

With White Beans

1 cucumber, peeled and diced

1 green bell pepper, diced

5 green onions, chopped

2 cloves garlic, minced

3 tomatoes, diced

2 stalks celery, diced

2½ cups canned cannellini beans, rinsed and drained

2 tablespoons olive oil

¼ cup red wine vinegar

5 cups tomato juice

1 teaspoon ground cumin

1 tablespoon fresh parsley, minced

1 tablespoon fresh basil, minced

½ tablespoon fresh oregano, minced

¼ teaspoon salt

Prepare all vegetables and place in a large bowl. Add all remaining ingredients.

Chill for at least one hour. Serve very cold.

MAKES 6 TO 8 SERVINGS

corn and crab chowder

5 medium thin-skinned potatoes

½ pound applewood-smoked bacon

2 cups celery, diced

2 cups yellow onions, diced

1 cup white wine

¼ cup cornstarch

1 teaspoon fresh-ground pepper

4 tablespoons sugar

½ teaspoon dried thyme

2 teaspoons nutmeg

1 teaspoon Old Bay seasoning

2 bay leaves

1 tablespoon dried dill

2 cups corn

½ cup seafood base
(see Resources)

1 quart plus 1 cup heavy cream

2 quarts plus 2 cups milk

1 pound crabmeat, cooked and cleaned

fresh parsley or fresh dill for garnish

Slice potatoes into ¼-inch cubes, cover with water and cook until tender. Set aside.

Cut bacon into ¼-inch pieces and sauté in a 5-quart saucepan until brown and slightly crispy. Chop celery and onions into ¼-inch dice and add to the pan and let them sweat for about 5 minutes. Add wine to deglaze the pan and cook for another minute.

In a separate bowl, mix together all the dry ingredients and add to the pan, stirring well. Add corn and cooked potatoes.

Add seafood base, cream and milk. Bring to a boil so the cornstarch can thicken the liquid, and the corn and potatoes are heated through. Remove from heat and stir in crabmeat. Garnish with fresh parsley or dill and serve with oyster crackers.

MAKES 8 TO 10 SERVINGS

carrot ginger soup

2 pounds carrots, chopped

¼ cup fresh ginger, grated

1 tablespoon garlic, minced

2 tablespoons butter

7 cups vegetable broth

1 cup Marsala wine

1 bay leaf

1 teaspoon each of
salt and white pepper

1 tablespoon brown sugar

¼ teaspoon allspice

⅛ teaspoon cinnamon

pinch ground cardamom

1 cup heavy cream

Fried Carrots
(see below)

CARROTS

2 large carrots,
julienne sliced

½ teaspoon sugar

¼ teaspoon salt

¼ teaspoon each ground
ginger and ground cumin

¼ teaspoon New Mexican
chile powder
(see Resources)

1 cup oil

Melt butter in a medium saucepan, and sauté the ginger and garlic until the garlic is clear.

Add the vegetable broth, wine, bay leaf, salt, pepper and carrots to the pot. Add the brown sugar and spices. Bring to a boil, lower heat and cover. Simmer until the carrots are extremely tender, testing with a fork until it pierces the carrot easily.

While soup is cooking, prepare the Fried Carrots and set aside. Remove soup from heat and let cool. In batches, puree the soup until creamy. Return to pan, stir in cream, and taste for seasoning. Ladle soup into bowls and top with Fried Carrots.

MAKES 6 TO 8 SERVINGS

FRIED CARROTS

Mix together sugar, salt and spices. Heat oil in a deep pot. When very hot, add the julienned carrots, stirring so they do not stick together. Let cook until they turn a golden brown. Remove from oil and drain on paper towels.

Put warm carrots in a small bowl and sprinkle with mixed spices while tossing.

asparagus tarragon soup

¼ **cup butter**

2 **pounds asparagus, chopped**
(use fresh or frozen)

3 **cups chicken broth**

2 **cups half and half**

1 **cup dry white wine**

2 **teaspoons fresh tarragon, minced**

⅛ **teaspoon nutmeg**

1 **teaspoon each of salt and white pepper**

1 **cup Gruyère or Jarlsberg cheese, grated for garnish**

In a large pot, melt butter and lightly sauté the asparagus. Add all the remaining ingredients, except cheese, to the pot. Bring to a boil and lower heat so asparagus simmers until extremely tender, about 10 minutes. The soup may appear to separate but that will disappear when blended.

Remove from heat and let cool. In batches, puree the soup until creamy. Taste and adjust for seasoning.

Delicious hot or cold. For cold soup, garnish with asparagus spears. For hot soup, top with grated cheese and serve with French bread.

MAKES 6 SERVINGS

black bean soup

8 cups canned black beans

2 tablespoons canola oil

1 small onion, diced

1 medium carrot, diced small

2 medium potatoes, diced small

1 cup green chile, chopped

2 tablespoons masa harina or cornmeal for thickening

½ cup Lesley's Black Bean Spice
(see below)

5 cups vegetable broth

salt and pepper to taste

LESLEY'S BLACK BEAN SPICE

¼ cup ground fennel

¼ cup ground cumin

¼ cup New Mexican chile powder
(see Resources)

1 tablespoon dried oregano

½ tablespoon garlic powder

½ tablespoon onion powder

1 teaspoon sugar

1½ tablespoons salt

Drain and rinse beans and set aside. Heat oil in a medium saucepan. Add the onion, carrots and potatoes; sauté until the onions are translucent. Add the green chile, masa harina or cornmeal (if using cornmeal, mix with hot water and let it sit a bit before adding) and Black Bean Spice. Stir well until smooth.

Add the beans and vegetable broth, and stir until mixed well. Cover and bring the soup to a boil. Reduce heat and let cook until the potatoes and carrots are tender. Adjust taste with salt and pepper.

Ladle into bowls and top with a dollop of Mexican crema or sour cream, sliced avocado, chopped cilantro and your favorite salsa.

MAKES 10 SERVINGS

LESLEY'S BLACK BEAN SPICE
Mix together all ingredients and store in a cool, dry place.

MAKES 1 CUP

FOR A HEARTY STEW
Add 1 pound pre-cooked sausage (I like to use chorizo) and top with 1 cup grated Cheddar cheese and ½ cup sliced green onions.

salads and dressings

lesley's herb vinaigrette

2 cups salad oil,
preferably canola

⅔ cup extra virgin olive oil

⅔ cup white wine vinegar

4 tablespoons
balsamic vinegar

1 tablespoon lemon juice

4 tablespoons orange juice

¼ cup sugar

1 teaspoon garlic powder

1 teaspoon dried oregano

1 teaspoon kosher salt

1 tablespoon
cracked pepper

pinch of cayenne

½ cup mixed fresh herbs
thyme, basil,
parsley and mint
*(do not use fresh sage
or rosemary)*

This recipe is my basic vinaigrette and is wonderful for any salad that calls for classic vinaigrette dressing. It can be enhanced in many different ways, depending on what ingredients are in your salad. The Citrus, Cranberry and Strawberry versions are examples of how this basic recipe can be expanded — use your imagination to create your own special vinaigrette.

Combine the oils and set aside. Put all ingredients except the oils in a blender or food processor and mix until smooth.

Slowly add the combined oils to thicken dressing. If it gets too thick, remove from the blender or food processor, pour into a bowl and finish adding the oil. Continue to whisk by hand.

Pour into an airtight container and refrigerate. It will last for up to a month.

MAKES 3 CUPS

Vinaigrette Variations

CITRUS

2 cups of Herb Vinaigrette

¼ cup each, grapefruit and orange juice

⅛ cup sweet Thai chili sauce
(see Resources)

⅛ cup loose mint and cilantro leaves

salt and pepper to taste

CRANBERRY

1 cup Herb Vinaigrette

¼ cup cranberry juice

⅛ cup dried cranberries

⅛ teaspoon each harissa and garam masala
(see Resources or page 199 and 198)

⅛ teaspoon ground ginger

⅛ teaspoon fresh mint leaves, chopped

pinch cinnamon

STRAWBERRY

1 cup Herb Vinaigrette

½ cup fresh strawberries

1 tablespoon fresh basil, chopped

1 teaspoon fresh lemon juice

½ teaspoon garam masala
(see Resources or page 198)

salt and pepper to taste

CITRUS VINAIGRETTE

Combine all ingredients in a blender and mix until smooth. Dressing will keep in a sealed container in the refrigerator for up to one month.

MAKES 2½ CUPS

CRANBERRY VINAIGRETTE

Combine all ingredients in a blender and mix until smooth. Dressing will keep in a sealed container in the refrigerator for up to one month.

MAKES 1 CUP

STRAWBERRY VINAIGRETTE

Combine all ingredients in a blender and mix until smooth. Refrigerate and use within 24 hours.

MAKES 1½ CUPS

graham's greens

With Chile Pepitas and Cotija Cheese

1 head romaine,
chopped

½ cup red cabbage,
shredded

4 radishes, julienned

½ cup jicama, julienned

1 tablespoon
chile pepitas
(see below)

1 teaspoon Cotija
cheese, grated

PEPITAS

2 cups pumpkin seeds

¼ cup canola oil

1 tablespoon New Mexican
red chile powder
(see Resources)

¼ teaspoon cumin

½ teaspoon salt

Wash and prepare vegetables. Mix together in a bowl and
toss gently with Lesley's Herb Vinaigrette *(see page 66)*.
Sprinkle pepitas and cheese on top and serve immediately.

MAKES 4 SERVINGS

CHILE PEPITAS (PUMPKIN SEEDS)

Preheat oven to 350°F. Place pumpkin seeds in a small
bowl; add oil and toss. Combine seasonings and sprinkle
on pumpkin seeds. Toss again.

Spread seeds on a cookie sheet and bake for about 10
minutes, stirring frequently to prevent burning. Store in
an airtight container.

MAKES 2 CUPS

bacon and bleu salad

1 cup Bleu Cheese Dressing
(see below)

**4 strips applewood-
smoked bacon**

1 head of romaine lettuce

1 medium tomato, diced

DRESSING
2½ teaspoons lemon juice

½ teaspoon dried mustard

½ teaspoon salt

pinch of black pepper

pinch of cayenne pepper

1¾ tablespoons olive oil

**1 teaspoon
Worcestershire sauce**

dash of Tabasco

**⅔ cup bleu, Roquefort
or Gorgonzola cheese,
crumbled**
reserving some for garnish

⅔ cup mayonnaise

⅔ cup sour cream

**2 tablespoons
heavy cream**

**1 tablespoon
cider vinegar**

Prepare the Bleu Cheese Dressing and refrigerate until ready to use. Cook the bacon, drain on paper towels and chop or crumble into small pieces.

Wash, core and remove any damaged outside leaves from lettuce. Slice into 4 sections vertically. Dice the tomato.

Have 4 plates ready. Lay the sliced romaine on the plates cut side up. Pour Bleu Cheese Dressing over the middle of the romaine. Top with diced tomatoes, bleu cheese crumbles and chopped cooked bacon.

Makes 4 servings

Bleu Cheese Dressing
Pulse all ingredients in food processor until nicely chunky or mix by hand in a bowl. Pour into an airtight container and refrigerate. Dressing can be stored for up to one month.

Makes 2 cups

ensenada shrimp salad

1¼ cups Citrus Vinaigrette
(see page 67)

**1 pound medium shrimp,
cooked, peeled
and deveined**

¼ cup Savory Spice Mix
(see page 194)

**1 pink grapefruit or
1 cup grapefruit sections***

**2 oranges or
1 cup orange sections***

**1 small sweet red onion,
sliced thin**

2 avocados, sliced

**¼ cup Cotija
cheese, grated**

**2 heads of butter or
romaine lettuce**

Prepare the Citrus Vinaigrette and set aside. Prepare the shrimp and season with Savory Spice Mix. Segment the oranges and grapefruit, and thinly slice the onion. Cut the avocado in half, remove pit, scoop out flesh with a spoon and cut into slices.

Grate the Cotija cheese and tear lettuce into large pieces. Divide lettuce among 8 plates or large bowls. Add citrus, shrimp, avocado and onion. Pour dressing over salads and sprinkle with Cotija cheese.

MAKES 8 SERVINGS

These orange and grapefruit sections are now available in nearly all supermarkets in the refrigerated produce department; if you prefer, you can peel and section from the whole fruit.

BBQ cobb salad

1 cup Chipotle BBQ Ranch Dressing
(see right)

8 strips applewood-smoked bacon

8 ounces boneless chicken breasts

½ cup roasted corn*
(see right)

½ cup green chile, diced

1 head butter or romaine lettuce

1 medium tomato, diced

4 ounces Monterey Jack cheese, cubed

¼ cup jicama, julienned

2 small radishes, sliced

1 avocado, diced

blue corn chips
(optional)

Prepare Chipotle BBQ Ranch Dressing and refrigerate until ready to use. Cook bacon until crisp; drain on paper towels and chop or cut with scissors into small pieces.

Cut chicken breasts into cubes, season with salt and pepper and sauté in the leftover bacon fat. Remove and drain on paper towels.

Prepare corn and tear lettuce into bite-size pieces.

In a large mixing bowl, toss lettuce with Chipotle BBQ Ranch Dressing. Begin with ¼ cup and add more if needed. Add remaining ingredients except avocado and blue corn chips and toss again lightly.

Mound mixture on salad plates or bowls; add diced avocado and serve with extra dressing and blue corn chips on the side.

MAKES 4 SERVINGS

chipotle BBQ ranch dressing

1 packet Hidden Valley Ranch Buttermilk Dressing

1 cup buttermilk

1 cup mayonnaise

½ cup BBQ sauce
(your favorite kind)

2 tablespoons chipotle in adobo sauce, pureed
(add more chipotle if you like it hot)

Follow the directions on the packet of Hidden Valley dressing, using the buttermilk and mayonnaise listed in the ingredients. Put dressing, BBQ sauce and chipotle in adobo sauce into a stand-up mixer and mix well. Chill for at least one hour before dressing salad.

MAKES 2½ CUPS

*Roasting corn: Have ears of corn shucked and cleaned. Oil lightly and place on a hot grill. Turn until all sides get a light brown char to parts of the kernels. You do not have to char all of the kernels. Cool and place in refrigerator. When chilled, slice off the kernels with a sharp knife, going vertically against the kernels.

If using frozen corn, thaw kernels and drain. Place on a cookie sheet and put into a preheated oven at 300°F. Reduce heat to 250°F and roast slowly to dry the corn slightly and bring out the sweetness of the kernels.

beet, radicchio and spinach

With Goat Cheese Fritters and Pistachios

6 beets, cooked with the skins on then peeled

18 Goat Cheese Fritters

1 cup Candied Pistachios

1½ cups Citrus Vinaigrette
(see page 67)

1 large (12-ounce) bag of spinach

1 head of radicchio, sliced

You can roast the beets and prepare the fritters and pistachios the day before.

Preheat oven to 425°F. Scrub beets and poke them with a fork a couple of times. Put in the oven and roast for 45 to 60 minutes until done and they pierce easily with a fork. Cooking time depends on the size of the beets, so start checking them after 30 minutes. When done, remove from oven and let them cool.

When beets have cooled, put on a pair of gloves and peel. Gloves will protect your hands from staining. Put peeled beets in a sealed container and refrigerate until ready to use.

Prepare the Goat Cheese Fritters and put in the refrigerator to chill.

Reduce oven temperature to 300°F and prepare Candied Pistachios; let cool. Prepare the Citrus Vinaigrette.

When ready to serve, slice the roasted beets, put the spinach and radicchio in a large bowl and toss with Citrus Vinaigrette. Divide the spinach mix among 6 plates and top with sliced beets, Goat Cheese Fritters and Candied Pistachios.

MAKES 6 SERVINGS

FRITTERS

2 cups goat cheese

¾ cup cream cheese
(at room temperature)

**1 tablespoon each of fresh
mint and basil, minced**

**pinch each of nutmeg,
salt and pepper**

1 egg

**¼ cup panko bread
crumbs for coating**

canola oil for frying

PISTACHIOS

1 cup pistachios

**2 tablespoons sweet
Thai chili sauce**
(see Resources)

dash of Sriracha sauce
(see Resources)

1 teaspoon vanilla extract

3 tablespoons sugar

2 teaspoons salt

¼ teaspoon cinnamon

GOAT CHEESE FRITTERS

Mix cheeses, herbs, spices and egg together in a food processor or by hand. Form into balls and flatten slightly to about 1-inch wide and ½-inch thick. Roll flattened patties in panko. Chill. When ready to use, fry in hot oil until light golden brown.

MAKES 18 FRITTERS

CANDIED PISTACHIOS

Heat oven to 300°F. Toss all ingredients together. Put nuts on a cookie sheet and bake for about 12 minutes, stirring often to prevent burning. Remove from oven and let cool.

MAKES 1 CUP

tijuana caesar salad

With Parmesan Scallops and Croutons

1½ cups Romano cheese,
freshly grated and divided

¾ cup panko bread crumbs

¼ teaspoon each dried
oregano, dried basil and salt

1 cup flour

1 egg

½ to ¾ pound of scallops,
(I love the U-10 big scallops)

1 cup canola oil
for frying scallops

1 large head of romaine,
halved or quartered

1 cup of Tijuana
Caesar Dressing
(see right)

1 cup Anchovy Croutons
(see right)

1 large red pepper,
roasted and julienned

Prepare Anchovy Croutons and set aside. Prepare Tijuana Caesar Dressing and refrigerate until ready to use.

Combine 1 cup of the Romano cheese with the panko, spices and salt and put on a small plate. Put all the flour on another small plate. Beat the egg in a small bowl.

Roll scallops in the flour, dip in the egg and roll in the panko-cheese-spice mixture and set aside.

Heat oil in a skillet large enough to cook all of the scallops. Put breaded scallops into the hot oil, flat side down and sear. Turn over and brown on the other side. Do not overcook; medium rare is best. You want the golden brown of a good sear but not the excess cooking time in the pan. Drain scallops on paper towels and let them rest.

Lay the romaine on the plates, halved for large salads or quartered for smaller ones. Top with dressing, remaining cheese and croutons; lastly, add the scallops and red pepper.

MAKES 2 LARGE OR 4 SMALL SALADS

2-3 anchovy fillets, minced

3 large cloves garlic, minced

2 cups day-old
French bread, cubed

3 tablespoons olive oil

¼ teaspoon ground
black pepper

DRESSING

4 egg yolks

⅓ teaspoon dried mustard

¾ tablespoon black pepper

¾ tablespoon salt

⅓ cup lemon juice

¼ cup white wine vinegar

⅛ cup anchovy paste

1¼ tablespoons
Worcestershire sauce

1 tablespoon fresh
parsley, chopped

2 cloves garlic

⅓ cup Parmesan
cheese, grated

¼ cup extra virgin
olive oil

¾ cups canola oil

ANCHOVY CROUTONS

Chop the anchovies, peel and chop the garlic, and cut French bread into cubes, leaving the crust.

Heat olive oil in a large skillet over medium heat. Add the anchovies and cook, stirring, until they melt into oil, about 2 minutes.

Add bread cubes and pepper. Toast in the pan, tossing frequently, until croutons are golden, 3 to 5 minutes.

Now stir in the garlic and cook, stirring, until fragrant and croutons turn a dark golden brown, 1 to 2 minutes. Immediately remove from pan and set aside.

MAKES 2 CUPS

TIJUANA CAESAR DRESSING

Combine all ingredients except oils in a blender on slow speed. Slowly add oils and continue blending until oil is emulsified and dressing thickens. Pour into container and refrigerate. Dressing can be stored for up to 1 month.

MAKES 2½ CUPS

Caesar salad was invented in 1924 in Tijuana, Mexico, by a man named Caesar Cardini (an Italian-born Mexican), who ran a restaurant and nightclub called "Caesar's Place." Cardini lived in San Diego but worked in Tijuana, where he could avoid the restrictions of Prohibition. Cardini did not add anchovies to his dressing, but all the Italians do!

popeye spinach salad

1 cup Spicy Sweet Chile Pecans
(see below)

1 (12-ounce) bag fresh spinach

1 carrot, julienned

½ cup dried cranberries

½ cup bleu, Roquefort or Gorgonzola cheese, crumbled

Cranberry Vinaigrette
(see page 67)

PECANS

¼ cup New Mexican red chile sauce
(see Resources)

¼ to 1 tablespoon Sriracha hot chili sauce,
depending on how hot you like it
(see Resources)

2 tablespoons sweet Thai chili sauce
(see Resources)

1 tablespoon vanilla

2 cups pecan halves

1 teaspoon cinnamon

¼ teaspoon each of nutmeg and allspice

½ tablespoon salt

1 tablespoon brown sugar

Prepare the Spicy Sweet Chile Pecans, and while they are cooling, you can wash and dry the spinach and julienne the carrot.

Mix the spinach and carrots, toss with the Cranberry Vinaigrette and divide among 4 plates. Top with cheese crumbles, pecans and dried cranberries.

MAKES 4 SERVINGS

SPICY SWEET CHILE PECANS

Preheat oven to 350°F. In a medium bowl, whisk together New Mexico chile sauce, Sriracha sauce, Thai chili sauce and vanilla. Add pecan halves and toss well.

Sprinkle nuts with remaining spices and sugar and toss again. Taste to adjust seasonings with salt or sugar.

Spread nuts in a single layer on a cookie sheet and bake for about 12 minutes. Toss them in the pan every 2-3 minutes to prevent burning, especially at the edges. When done, they will be fragrant and a deep golden brown.

After cooling, store in a sealed container. They will get crispier as they cool. Great for snacks, green salads and fruit salads.

MAKES 2 CUPS

moroccan shrimp salad

½ cup Spiced Almonds
(see below)

1 cup Moroccan
French Dressing
(see right)

8 spears fresh asparagus

½ cup fresh fennel, slivered

½ cup dried apricot, slivered

2 heads hearts of
romaine lettuce

1 pound of shrimp, cooked,
peeled and deveined

ALMONDS

2 cups blanched
whole almonds

1 tablespoon melted butter

⅛ cup sweet Thai Chile sauce
(see Resources)

dash of Sriracha sauce
(see Resources)

½ teaspoon vanilla extract

1 tablespoon harissa
(see Resources or page 199)

1 tablespoon ras el hanout
(see Resources or page 211)

3 tablespoons sugar

2 teaspoons salt

Prepare Spiced Almonds and Moroccan French Dressing.

Peel the asparagus then bend to snap off stems. Cook in boiling water for 2-3 minutes, until tender and immediately immerse in ice-cold water to stop cooking. Set aside.

Cut the fennel in half, remove the core and cut into slivers. Use scissors to cut the dried apricot into slivers.

Cut the romaine into 4 wedges, lengthwise from top to bottom, and place on serving plates. Drizzle the dressing over the romaine and top each wedge with shrimp, fennel, asparagus, apricots and Spiced Almonds. Garnish with a fresh or preserved lemon slice *(see Resources)*. Serve with warm French bread and butter and extra dressing on the side.

MAKES 4 SERVINGS

SPICED ALMONDS
Heat oven to 350°F. Toss all ingredients together. Place on a cookie sheet in the oven and bake until golden brown, about 12 minutes, turning frequently to prevent burning. Let cool.

½ cup white wine vinegar

1 tablespoon minced
preserved lemon or
1 tablespoon lemon juice

1 teaspoon herbs
de Provence

1 teaspoon anchovy paste

½ teaspoon harissa
(see Resources or page 199)

1 teaspoon French mustard
(Grey Poupon or similar)

1 teaspoon fresh mint

½ teaspoon toasted cumin

1 tablespoon sugar

1 cup extra virgin olive oil

Moroccan French Dressing

Combine all ingredients except olive oil in a blender or
food processor and blend well. Slowly add the olive oil
until dressing is smooth and thick. Taste for sweetness
and add salt and pepper if desired.

Makes 2 cups

strawberry spinach salad

With Spicy Pecans and Feta Cheese

1 cup Spicy Sweet Chile Pecans
(see right)

1½ cups Strawberry Vinaigrette
(see page 67)

1 carrot, julienned

1 pound fresh strawberries, sliced

1 (12-ounce) bag baby spinach leaves

1 cup feta or goat cheese, crumbled

Prepare Spicy Sweet Chile Pecans and Strawberry Vinaigrette and set aside.

Divide spinach into 8 large salad bowls. Top with strawberries, carrots, crumbled cheese and pecans and drizzle with Strawberry Vinaigrette.

MAKES 8 LARGE SALADS

PECANS

¼ **cup New Mexican red chile sauce**
(see Resources)

¼ **to 1 tablespoon Sriracha hot chili sauce**
depending on how hot you like it
(see Resources)

2 **tablespoons sweet Thai chili sauce**
(see Resources)

1 **tablespoon vanilla**

2 **cups pecan halves**

1 **teaspoon cinnamon**

¼ **teaspoon each of nutmeg and allspice**

½ **tablespoon salt**

1 **tablespoon brown sugar**

SPICY SWEET CHILE PECANS

Preheat oven to 350°F. In a medium bowl, whisk together New Mexican chile sauce, Sriracha sauce, Thai chili sauce, and vanilla. Add pecan halves and toss well.

Sprinkle nuts with remaining spices and sugar and toss again. Taste to adjust seasonings with salt or sugar.

Spread nuts in a single layer on a cookie sheet and bake for about 12 minutes. Toss them in the pan every 2-3 minutes to prevent burning, especially at the edges. When done, they will be fragrant and a deep golden brown.

After cooling, store in a sealed container. They will get crispier as they cool. Great for snacks, green salads and fruit salads.

MAKES 2 CUPS

sandwiches

triple c chicken sandwich

1 cup Chipotle Mayonnaise
(see below)

1 pound chicken breasts,
cooked and diced

⅛ cup green chile, chopped

8 slices of firm bread,
like ciabatta

½ to ¾ cup Chipotle
Mayonnaise for
spreading on bread
(optional)

1 avocado, sliced

¼ head lettuce, shredded

1 tomato, sliced

salt and pepper to taste

MAYONNAISE

2 cups mayonnaise

3 tablespoons chipotle in
adobo sauce, pureed

1 teaspoon cumin

1¾ teaspoons lime juice

⅓ teaspoon oregano

2 tablespoons
green chile, chopped

pinch black pepper

pinch salt

With Chipotle Mayonnaise

Prepare Chipotle Mayonnaise. Combine diced chicken, Chipotle Mayonnaise and chopped green chile in a bowl; mix well.

Toast the bread, lay out 4 slices and spread each slice with the extra Chipotle Mayonnaise.

Scoop chicken mixture onto each slice and add the sliced avocado, lettuce and tomato. Season with salt and pepper and top with remaining bread.

MAKES 4 SANDWICHES

CHIPOTLE MAYONNAISE

Combine all ingredients and mix well. Leftover mayonnaise will keep in the refrigerator for 30 days. Can be used to spice up other sandwiches, like tuna salad.

MAKES 3 CUPS

taos cheese steak

With Green Chile

1 cup Lesley's Famous
Three Cheese Sauce
(see page 28)

1 pound beef steak

1 tablespoon olive oil

4 jalapeños, seeded,
deveined and halved

1 yellow onion, sliced

1 red bell pepper,
julienned

4 whole roasted Hatch or
Anaheim green chiles,
peeled and seeded
*(see Tips, how to
roast chile on page 221)*

4 French or
sourdough rolls

½ cup Cotija
cheese, grated

Prepare Lesley's Famous Three Cheese Sauce and set aside, but keep warm. Salt and pepper steak and grill to your liking.

While steak is grilling, put a large skillet on high heat. Add olive oil and sauté jalapeños, onion and red pepper until golden.

Put roasted green chile on top of steak to warm. Slice rolls and grill, cut side down.

When steak is done, remove from heat and let rest for about 2 minutes. Slice steak into thin strips; divide among the 4 sandwiches. Top steak with cheese sauce, sautéed vegetables and Cotija cheese.

MAKES 4 SANDWICHES

salmon burgers

1 cup Green Chile
Tartar Sauce
(see below)

1½ pounds boneless,
skinless salmon

2 teaspoons
Dijon mustard

2 shallots, chopped

½ cup panko
bread crumbs

1 tablespoon capers,
chopped

salt and pepper to taste

¼ cup olive oil

6 burger buns

GARNISH

sliced tomatoes

shredded lettuce

SAUCE

2 cups mayonnaise

¼ cup green
chile, chopped

2 teaspoons fresh
cilantro, chopped

1 teaspoon red
onion, diced

1 teaspoon
fresh lime juice

Prepare Green Chile Tartar Sauce. Cut salmon into chunks. Put half of the salmon into a food processor with the mustard and grind until pasty.

Add shallots and the rest of the salmon, pulsing into a puree. In a medium bowl, combine bread crumbs, capers, salt and pepper; add salmon-shallot puree. Mix well by hand or with a large spoon, and form into 6 equal patties.

Heat oil in a large skillet, when oil is hot, add patties and cook for about 3 minutes on each side.

Serve on burger buns with Green Chile Tartar Sauce, tomatoes and lettuce.

MAKES 6 BURGERS

GREEN CHILE TARTAR SAUCE
Combine all ingredients in a medium bowl and mix together, adjusting for taste with salt and pepper.

MAKES 2¼ CUPS

hot damn crab burgers

1 tablespoon chipotle
in adobo sauce, pureed

⅓ cup mayonnaise

1 egg

2 tablespoons honey

1 tablespoon lime juice

pinch each salt,
pepper and
ground cumin

¾ pound snow crab,
drained

¼ cup green onions,
sliced thin

¼ cup cilantro, minced

2½ cups panko
bread crumbs

2 cups canola oil

8 slices
sourdough bread

butter for
toasting bread

16 slices sharp
Cheddar cheese

2 large tomatoes, sliced

Mix chipotle in adobo sauce with mayonnaise, egg, honey, lime juice and spices in a food processor or blender.

In a large bowl, mix together the crab, onions, cilantro and mayonnaise mixture with 1½ cups of the panko. If the mixture feels too wet, add a little more panko. Let mixture rest in the refrigerator for at least 4 hours.

Using a scoop or spoon, form the mixture into 8 patties and coat them with the remaining panko. Heat oil in a skillet, and when hot, add the patties and cook until golden brown, about 3 minutes on each side.

Turn on the broiler and butter one side of each sourdough slice. Put the bread, buttered side up, on a cookie sheet and put under the broiler until golden brown. Flip the bread over and top with one slice of Cheddar cheese; put the cookie sheet back under the broiler briefly to melt the cheese.

Place a crab patty on top of the melted cheese and add another slice of cheese. Return to the oven to melt the cheese. Top with a slice of tomato and serve open face.

MAKES 8 SANDWICHES

lamb burger

⅛ cup fresh mint, minced

⅛ cup fresh cilantro, minced

1½ tablespoons cumin

1 tablespoon New Mexico red chile powder
(see Resources)

⅛ cup garlic, minced

1 tablespoon salt

½ tablespoon black pepper

2 eggs

1¼ cups panko bread crumbs

2 pounds ground lamb

6 burger size buns
(a firm roll like ciabatta works well)

sliced tomato and lettuce for garnish

AIOLI

1 fresh lemon

2 cups mayonnaise

½ tablespoon dried garlic

1 tablespoon dried parsley

pinch each salt, black pepper and sugar

With Lemon Parsley Aioli

Prepare Lemon Parsley Aioli. Combine all ingredients except the ground lamb in a large bowl and mix thoroughly; add the lamb and mix again.

Form patties and grill for 8-10 minutes over direct medium heat, until lamb reaches medium rare, 140°F on a meat thermometer. While lamb is grilling, cut buns in half and toast in the oven.

Serve burgers on the toasted buns with tomato, lettuce and a dollop of Lemon Parsley Aioli.

Makes 8 (6-ounce) burgers

LEMON PARSLEY AIOLI
Zest and juice lemon. Combine all ingredients and let set for at least one hour before serving.

If not enough lemon for your taste, add more. I use a lemon concentrate made by Nielsen's Citrus that you can buy online *(see Resources)*. Refrigerate aioli in an airtight container for up to one month.

Makes 2½ cups

tenderloin steak sandwich

With Bleu Cheese Butter

½ cup **Bleu Cheese Butter**
(see right)

1 red onion,
sliced ½-inch-thick

¾ cup tawny port,
divided

1 teaspoon olive oil

4 beef tenderloin steaks,
2 -3 ounces each

2 tablespoons walnut
or vegetable oil

1 large beefsteak
tomato, sliced
¼-inch-thick

4 French or
sourdough burger
buns, sliced

salt and pepper to taste

Prepare Bleu Cheese Butter and refrigerate. Lay onion slices in a single layer on a cookie sheet. Drizzle with 2 tablespoons port and 1 teaspoon olive oil.

Place steaks in a 1-gallon plastic bag. Pour remaining port and walnut or vegetable oil over meat; seal bag and turn to coat. Let marinate at least 30 minutes, or up to 2 hours in the refrigerator.

Remove steaks from marinade and place on an oiled barbecue grill over medium coals or at medium heat on a gas grill. Lay onion slices around steaks and close the lid.

Cook steaks, turning once, until browned and done to your liking, about 12 minutes for medium-rare. Cook onions, turning once, until lightly browned on both sides, approximately 15 minutes. Remove steaks and onions from the grill and let rest for 5 minutes.

While steaks and onions are resting, grill buns on cut side until grill marks show. Remove bread from grill and spread both top and bottom with Bleu Cheese Butter.

Cut the steaks into thin slices against the grain and place the sliced steak on the bun (one steak for each sandwich); top with a large tomato slice. Sprinkle with salt and pepper, then top with grilled onions. Cut sandwiches in half and serve immediately.

MAKES 4 SANDWICHES

1 pound butter, softened

¼ pound bleu or Roquefort cheese, crumbled

¼ cup fresh parsley, chopped

1 teaspoon fresh-ground black pepper

salt to taste

BLEU CHEESE BUTTER

Mix together all ingredients in a bowl or food processor and chill, covered, until needed. Excellent on grilled meats or pasta.

MAKES 1¼ POUNDS

roast lamb sandwich

With Mint Chimichurri Sauce

4 tablespoons
Mint Chimichurri Sauce
(see below)

4 French rolls

1 pound of roasted,
sliced lamb meat

2 tablespoons
beef broth

8 tablespoons
mayonnaise

½ head radicchio,
shredded thin

SAUCE

1½ cups fresh mint
leaves, loosely packed

¼ cup each fresh oregano
and cilantro leaves,
loosely packed

2 tablespoons
extra virgin olive oil

1½ tablespoons
fresh lime juice

1 tablespoon honey

1 teaspoon jalapeño,
minced

½ teaspoon salt

½ teaspoon fresh-
ground black pepper

1 clove garlic

Prepare Mint Chimichurri Sauce and set aside. Slice fresh rolls in half and heat in warm oven for 5 minutes.

While bread is heating, place lamb in a large skillet with beef broth. Do not boil; heat just until warm.

Spread rolls with mayonnaise on each side and top with Chimichurri Sauce. Divide lamb among sandwiches; top with shredded radicchio. Put top on sandwich and slice in half. Serve with extra Chimichurri Sauce on the side.

MAKES 4 SERVINGS

MINT CHIMICHURRI SAUCE
Combine all ingredients in a blender and pulse until coarsely chopped.

MAKES 1 CUP

shrimp torta

With Cilantro Mayonnaise

½ cup Cilantro
Mayonnaise
(see below)

½ cup Lesley's
Frijoles Negros
(see page 213)

1 pound shrimp

2 fresh jalapeños,
chopped

1 tomato, sliced

1 cup iceberg lettuce,
shredded

1 avocado, sliced

4 bolillo rolls

¼ pound Monterey
Jack cheese, shredded

GARNISH

1 lime to squeeze
over tortas

¼ cup Cotija cheese

hot sauce, your favorite

MAYONNAISE

½ cup Mexican crema
or sour cream

½ cup mayonnaise

¼ to ½ cup fresh
cilantro, chopped

1 tablespoon lime juice

Bolillo is a type of savory bread traditionally made in Mexico. It's a variation of the baguette (which can be substituted) and is often baked in an horno (a traditional Native American outdoor mud oven). If you can't find it in your supermarket, check your local Mexican grocery.

Prepare the Cilantro Mayonnaise and Frijoles Negros and set aside. Peel, devein and cook the shrimp (they can be grilled or boiled) and keep them warm. Prepare the vegetables.

Slice open the rolls and cover both sides with the shredded Monterey Jack cheese. Put the rolls under the broiler or in a 350°F oven to melt the cheese.

Layer the sandwiches with Frijoles Negros, shrimp, Cilantro Mayonnaise and all of the vegetables. Squeeze lime juice over the sandwich and top with crumbled Cotija cheese. Put top and bottom together and cut in half. Serve with extra Cilantro Mayonnaise, your favorite hot sauce and the remaining Frijoles Negros.

MAKES 4 TORTAS

CILANTRO MAYONNAISE
Mix all ingredients together, blending well. Set aside.

MAKES 1 CUP

new orleans muffuletta

Ham and Provolone Sandwich

½ cup Muffuletta Olive Salad
(see below)

1 large muffuletta bread

½ pound each smoked ham,
and salami, deli sliced

½ pound mozzarella
cheese, deli sliced

½ cup Parmesan cheese,
grated, plus extra
for garnish

fresh parsley for garnish

hot red chili flakes
for garnish

OLIVE SALAD

¼ cup red wine vinegar

2 cloves garlic, minced

1 teaspoon each dried
oregano and dried basil

⅓ cup olive oil

½ cup each large green olives,
and kalamata olives, sliced

½ cup peperoncini, chopped

½ cup roasted red pepper,
chopped

2 anchovies, chopped, or
1 tablespoon anchovy paste

1 tablespoon sugar

salt and fresh-ground black
pepper to taste

Muffuletta bread is a type of round Sicilian sesame bread, as well as a submarine-style sandwich that originated in New Orleans, Louisiana. If you can't find muffuletta bread, use a loaf of large, round French bread. If the bread does not have seeds, brush with an egg wash (1 egg mixed with 1 tablespoon milk), sprinkle with sesame seeds, and toast in a 350°F oven for 8 minutes.

Prepare Muffuletta Olive Salad. Heat oven to 350°F and slice muffuletta bread in half horizontally. Layer each side first with mozzarella then Parmesan cheese. Heat in oven until cheese is soft.

Layer ham and salami on each side and top with Muffuletta Olive Salad. Return sandwich, open face, to oven until toasty, 3 to 5 minutes.

Sprinkle sandwiches with a little more Parmesan cheese and fresh parsley. Put sandwich halves together and cut into four portions. Serve with extra Muffuletta Olive Salad, Parmesan cheese and hot red chili flakes.

MAKES 4 SANDWICHES

MUFFULETTA OLIVE SALAD
Mix all ingredients together and refrigerate for one hour or overnight. Let mixture come to room temperature when ready to serve.

MAKES 2 CUPS

best damn reuben

4 slices rye bread

butter for grilling

½ cup sauerkraut, drained

pinch caraway seed

Russian Dressing
(see right)

12 ounces precooked corned beef or pastrami, sliced thin

8 slices Swiss cheese

4 dill pickle planks

stone-ground mustard

If you are slicing the meat yourself, always go against the grain of the meat. The grain is easy to spot because it's the direction of the string-like fibers of the muscle. If you cut along the grain instead of against the grain, your meat will be tough and stringy.

You will need a flattop griddle, electric griddle or 2 large skillets for this recipe. Butter 4 slices of bread. Drain the sauerkraut and mix in a pinch of caraway seed. Make the Russian Dressing and put it the refrigerator to chill.

Heat the griddle or skillets and when hot, put on the sauerkraut and pastrami to warm. Reduce heat and turn frequently to prevent burning.

Lay the buttered bread on the other half of the griddle or in the other skillet. Place two slices of Swiss cheese on each piece of bread, making sure to cover the bread completely. The cheese works as a moisture barrier so the bread doesn't get mushy when you add the other ingredients. While the cheese is melting, put the pickles on the griddle to heat.

You are now ready to assemble the sandwiches. Leaving the bread on the griddle, stack ¼ of the meat on each of the 4 slices of bread, covering the melted cheese.

(continued)

DRESSING
1 cup mayonnaise
¼ cup ketchup
½ teaspoon prepared horseradish

Spread the Russian Dressing on top of the meat on 2 of the bread slices, and spread mustard on the other 2 slices. Top the meat and dressing with sauerkraut and the pickle planks. Put the other 2 slices of bread on top to form a sandwich. The bread should be nice and brown and the cheese melted.

Remove the sandwiches from the griddle, let rest for about 1 minute, slice in half and serve.

MAKES 2 SANDWICHES

RUSSIAN DRESSING
Mix all ingredients together and chill.

MAKES 1¼ CUPS

shrimp rice noodle wrap

½ cup Lime Ginger Soy Sauce
(see below)

½ cup Wasabi Ginger
Mayonnaise
(see below)

1 cup cooked rice noodles
or rice sticks, about 4 ounces

½ cup Chinese
cabbage, shredded

2 tablespoons scallions, minced

½ medium carrot, shredded

½ pound small
shrimp, cooked

4 (10-inch) flour tortillas

SOY SAUCE

1 teaspoon Thai fish sauce

2 teaspoons lime juice

2 teaspoons each fresh
cilantro, mint and basil, minced

½ teaspoon fresh ginger, grated

½ cup soy sauce

⅛ cup brown sugar

1 tablespoon cornstarch

½ teaspoon Chinese
five-spice powder

⅛ cup hoisin sauce

1 tablespoon sake

½ tablespoon rice vinegar

With Wasabi Ginger Mayonnaise

Prepare Lime Ginger Soy Sauce and Wasabi Ginger
Mayonnaise. Cook the rice noodles and toss with shredded
cabbage, scallions, carrots and Lime Ginger Soy Sauce.
Place 4 tortillas in microwave for 10 seconds, just to warm
so they are easier to roll.

Lay out tortillas and spread Wasabi Ginger Mayonnaise
over each one, then layer rice noodle mixture and shrimp.
Roll tight and even, like a sushi roll. Cut in half and serve
with extra Wasabi Mayonnaise and Lime Ginger Soy Sauce.

Makes 4 wraps

Lime Ginger Soy Sauce
Combine all ingredients in a saucepan and bring to a boil
to thicken. Let cool.

Makes ¾ cup

Wasabi Ginger Mayonnaise

1 cup mayonnaise

½ tablespoon fresh wasabi paste

1 tablespoon pickled ginger, chopped fine

Mix all ingredients in a small bowl and refrigerate for at least
one hour. Bring to room temperature when ready to use.

Makes 1 cup

tuna niçoise sandwich

1 cup Anchovy French Herb Mayonnaise
(see below)

1 large can albacore tuna white, drained

¼ cup pitted Niçoise olives, sliced

4 hardboiled eggs, sliced

¼ pound haricot verts

1 large French baguette

1 tomato, sliced

MAYONNAISE

1 tablespoon anchovy paste

1 cup mayonnaise

½ teaspoon fresh-ground pepper

1 teaspoon white wine vinegar

½ teaspoon herbs de Provence

Prepare the Anchovy French Herb Mayonnaise and mix with the tuna and Niçoise olives. Cook the haricot verts, rinse immediately with cold water to halt the cooking, and chill.

Slice the entire baguette in half lengthwise. Spread the tuna-olive mixture on one side of the bread. Layer the sliced eggs, haricot verts and sliced tomato on top of the tuna. Add salt and pepper to taste. Put baguette together and slice into 4 sections.

MAKES 4 SANDWICHES

ANCHOVY FRENCH HERB MAYONNAISE
Combine all ingredients in a small bowl and mix well. Refrigerate and let set for at least one hour. Return to room temperature before using.

MAKES 1 CUP

The name Niçoise comes from Nice, a city on the southeastern coast of France in the heart of the Riviera. The name is often mispronounced in American restaurants. Because of the e at the end of Niçoise, it's pronounced nee-SWAHZ, not nee-SWAH.

jamaican pork sandwich

With Mango Salsa, Fried Bananas and Peanuts

1 pound pork tenderloin, brined
(see right)

½ cup Lesley's Frijoles Negros
(see page 213)

½ cup Mango Salsa
(see right)

4 French rolls

butter for spreading

½ teaspoon sugar

½ cup canola oil

2 bananas

½ cup all-purpose flour

1 cup cabbage, chopped

¼ cup peanuts

4 tablespoons Pickapeppa Sauce
(see Resources)

24 hours before cooking pork, prepare brine and cure the meat.

Prepare Frijoles Negros and Mango Salsa.

Brush rolls with melted butter and sprinkle with sugar. Heat in oven for about 10 minutes. This is more like Jamaican bread.

Grill or sauté the pork; tenderloins are thin, so they cook quickly. Once pork is cooked, let it rest for about 5 minutes and slice thinly.

While pork is resting, pour oil into a large skillet. Let it get hot. Cut the bananas in half lengthwise and toss in the flour. Sauté bananas until they are golden brown; do not overcook. Remove from pan and drain on paper towels.

Slice bread in half lengthwise. Layer Frijoles Negros, pork, bananas, Mango Salsa, cabbage and peanuts; drizzle with Pickapeppa Sauce. Cut sandwiches in half before serving.

MAKES 4 SANDWICHES

SALSA

1 mango, diced

¼ cup red pepper, diced

2 tablespoons red onion, diced

1 jalapeño, diced

¼ cup mango puree
(see Resources)

salt and pepper to taste

lime juice to taste

BRINE

1½ cups water

⅓ cup plus 1 tablespoon sugar

⅛ cup salt

½ teaspoon red pepper flakes, crushed

1½ teaspoons black peppercorns

1½ teaspoons whole fennel seed

1 teaspoon dried thyme leaves

1 cup apple juice concentrate

½ tablespoon Chinese five-spice powder

½ tablespoon cinnamon

MANGO SALSA

Mix together all ingredients, adding only enough puree to hold the salsa together.

MAKES 1 CUP

PORK BRINE

Mix all ingredients together. Put pork tenderloin into a non-reactive container or plastic bag and pour brine over the meat. Brine for 24 to 96 hours in the refrigerator.

MAKES 3 CUPS

BBQ buffalo sandwich

1 cup Chipotle BBQ Sauce
(see right)

BUFFALO
2 cloves garlic, minced

2 teaspoons salt

1 tablespoon black pepper

2 large sprigs fresh
rosemary, chopped

4-pound boneless
buffalo chuck roast

1 cup red wine

2¼ cups beef broth, divided

SANDWICHES
8 slices Cheddar cheese

8 sesame burger buns, sliced
and toasted

16 dill pickle planks

2 tomatoes, sliced thin

1 sweet red onion, sliced thin

2 cups Chipotle BBQ Sauce

Prepare the Chipotle BBQ Sauce and set aside. Heat oven to 500°F. Combine the garlic, spices and fresh rosemary; rub all over the roast. Put the roast in a deep roasting pan; add red wine, 1¾ cups beef broth, and cover tightly with foil. As soon as you put the roast in the oven, immediately lower the temperature to 275°F. Cook covered for 2 hours, then uncover and cook 1 hour more.

Remove the buffalo roast from the oven and let cool for about an hour. Take meat out of the pan and scrape off any excess fat. Mix 1 cup of Chipotle BBQ Sauce together with the remaining ½ cup beef broth. Return meat to the pan and cover with sauce. Cover pan tightly with foil again and continue to cook for another 30 minutes. Remove from oven and let sit for about half an hour until the roast is cool enough to handle but not cold.

Remove meat from the pan and tear into shreds, about 1 inch by ½ inch. Mix the shredded meat with any sauce in the pan. You are now ready to make the sandwiches.

SANDWICHES
Put a slice of cheese on the bottom half of the bun. Place on a cookie sheet and put into oven at 350°F for 5 minutes. Remove from oven and put a big serving of buffalo on top of the melted cheese. Stack with tomatoes, pickles and red onions. Serve with a side of extra Chipotle BBQ sauce.

Makes 8 sandwiches

4 strips smoked bacon, chopped

½ cup onion, chopped

1 bottle dark beer

½ can (3.5-ounce) chipotle in adobo sauce, pureed

2 cups ketchup

¼ teaspoon liquid smoke

¼ cup dark brown sugar

6 cloves garlic, minced

½ cup cider vinegar

2 tablespoons thyme

2 tablespoons molasses

1 tablespoon black pepper

1 lime, zested and juiced

1½ teaspoons salt

1 teaspoon allspice

¼ teaspoon onion powder

⅛ teaspoon ground cinnamon

pinch ground cloves

⅓ stick of butter

SHORT VERSION

½ can (3.5-ounce) chipotle in adobo sauce, pureed

3 cups BBQ sauce

salt, pepper or sugar to taste

CHIPOTLE BBQ SAUCE (LONG VERSION)

Fry bacon until crisp. Add onions and cook for 5 minutes. Add beer and simmer for 5 minutes. Add all remaining ingredients except butter and bring to a boil. Slowly simmer for about 2 hours. Remove from heat, strain, stir in butter, and let cool. If you don't have time to make this sauce, use the short version below.

MAKES 3 CUPS

CHIPOTLE BBQ SAUCE (SHORT VERSION)

Mix together all ingredients and use just like the long version.

MAKES 3 CUPS

entrées

pink guava guajillo chicken

1 cup Pink Guava
Guajillo Sauce
(see below)

4 boneless chicken breasts

4 green chile cheese tamales
(see Resources)

2 cups New Mexican
green chile sauce
(see page 202)

4 cups Lesley's
Frijoles Negros
(see page 213)

1 cup Monterey Jack
cheese, shredded

¼ cup Cotija cheese, grated

SAUCE

2 cups Pink Guava Puree
(see Resources)

1 tablespoon ground
guajillo chili pepper
(see Resources)

1 cup white wine

1 tablespoon cornstarch

1 tablespoon chicken base
(see Resources)

salt and pepper to taste

Prepare Pink Guava Guajillo Sauce and set aside. Season chicken with salt and pepper and grill over direct medium heat for 8-12 minutes, turning often.

While the chicken is cooking, steam tamales on the stove in a steamer for 10-12 minutes, or if you are in a hurry, you can wrap the tamales in a wet towel and microwave until hot, about 3-4 minutes.

Heat chile sauce on the stovetop. Prepare black beans and heat until warmed through. Use oven-safe plates and put a spoonful of black beans in the middle of each plate. Top with a tamale, green chile sauce, Monterey Jack cheese and put in the oven to melt the cheese.

Remove from oven and add a chicken breast to each plate. Spoon warm Pink Guava Sauce over everything and top it with Cotija cheese. Serve with fried Serrano chiles, cilantro and your favorite vegetables.

MAKES 4 SERVINGS

PINK GUAVA GUAJILLO SAUCE
Whisk together all ingredients and cook until slightly thickened. Taste to adjust salt and pepper. This sauce is great over grilled chicken and excellent served with enchiladas or tamales and black beans.

MAKES 3 CUPS

honeyed white sea bass

Greek Style

2 pounds white sea bass
(If you don't have white sea bass, use large shrimp or another firm-fleshed fish)

**½ cup olive oil
(plus extra if needed
for sautéing)**

4 tablespoons honey

**2 tablespoons
Asian fish sauce or
4 tablespoons
Worcestershire sauce**

1 tablespoon garlic powder

**1 cup all-purpose flour
for dusting**
(for gluten free use rice flour)

**¾ cup Greek ouzo or
any anise-flavored liqueur**

**6 cups spinach,
steamed or sautéed**

3 cups rice, cooked

**½ cup roasted red peppers,
cut into ¼-inch strips**

**1 tablespoon fresh oregano
leaves, chopped**

fresh-ground black pepper

Cut fish steaks into large cubes, about 1½ inches. Mix ½ cup olive oil, honey and fish sauce together, whisking vigorously for about a minute.

Heat a large frying pan over high heat for 1-2 minutes. Add most of the oil mixture (a little more than half) and reserve the remainder. Turn heat down to medium high and heat the oil for 2 minutes.

Mix garlic powder with flour; dust the fish with seasoned flour, shaking off excess, and sear in the oil. Try to sear all 4 sides. Cook in batches if necessary, setting the finished fish aside to drain on paper towels as you do the rest. Add more of the olive oil as needed.

Pour ouzo into the pan and scrape up browned bits with a wooden spoon. Add the olive oil, honey and fish sauce mixture to the pan and mix everything well. Let this cook down until the whole surface of the pan is a mass of bubbles. Turn off heat and add the fish back to the pan and coat with sauce.

Spread the steamed or sautéed spinach evenly on serving plates and top with a ½ cup scoop of rice, fish and sauce. Garnish with the red pepper strips, chopped oregano leaves and black pepper.

MAKES 6 SERVINGS

turkey tenderloin

With Cranberry Mojo Sauce

2 cups Cranberry Mojo Sauce
(see next page)

6 (6-ounce) turkey tenderloins
(Turkey tenderloins are the long, tender strips of white meat hidden under the turkey breast. This is the same type of tenderloin used for fried chicken strips).

6 tablespoons vegetable oil

pinch each of salt, pepper and allspice

¼ pound butter

2 whole sweet potatoes, baked, peeled and sliced

pinch of salt, pepper and brown sugar

Prepare Cranberry Mojo Sauce and set aside. Prepare sweet potatoes.

Rub turkey tenderloins with oil, salt, pepper and allspice. Put on a hot grill and cook until medium well (150-155°F internal temperature). Remove from grill and let rest.

Heat a large skillet, melt butter and add sliced sweet potatoes, salt, pepper and a pinch of brown sugar. Turn often until slightly caramelized.

Divide sweet potatoes between 4 plates. Slice turkey tenderloin and put next to sweet potatoes, topping with warm Cranberry Mojo Sauce.

MAKES 6 SERVINGS

CRANBERRY MOJO SAUCE

1 cup cranberry sauce

½ cup cranberries

¼ cup cranberry juice

¼ cup orange juice

1 teaspoon lime juice

½ shallot, minced

1 clove garlic, minced

large pinch each cinnamon, nutmeg and allspice

½ teaspoon each Jamaican jerk seasoning and garam masala
(see Resources or page 198)

½ tablespoon New Mexican red chile powder
(see Resources)

¼ cup sugar

¼ cup tequila

salt and pepper to taste

Combine all ingredients in a large saucepan. Bring to a boil and continue to simmer for 1 hour, until cranberries are tender. Taste and adjust seasoning with salt and pepper.

MAKES 2 CUPS

my mom's meatloaf

¾ **pound each ground beef and ground pork**

1 **medium onion, diced**

2 **cloves garlic, minced**

1 **carrot, grated**

2 **tablespoons parsley, chopped**

2 **large eggs**

¼ **cup panko bread crumbs**

⅛ **cup Worcestershire sauce**

⅛ **cup Pickapeppa Sauce**
(see Resources)

⅛ **cup ketchup**

1 **teaspoon dry mustard**

¼ **teaspoon dried thyme**

¼ **teaspoon dried oregano**

¼ **teaspoon dried basil**

1½ **teaspoons coarse salt**

1 **teaspoon fresh-ground black pepper**

SAUCE (OPTIONAL)

1 **cup Pickapeppa Sauce**
(see Resources)

1 **cup ketchup**

pinch fresh-ground pepper

Preheat oven to 375°F degrees. Combine all ingredients in a large bowl, mix well and let set for 10 minutes. Remove meat mixture from bowl and place on a cookie sheet, mounding into 1 or 2 loaves. Cover each loaf with foil and put into the oven.

If making 1 large loaf, bake for 30 minutes, remove foil and continue baking for another 30 minutes. If making 2 smaller loaves, remove the foil after 25 minutes and continue baking for 20 minutes more. Meat loaf is done when a meat thermometer inserted into the center of the loaf reads 160°F.

MAKES 8 TO 10 SERVINGS

SAUCE
Mix the sauce ingredients together and heat in a small saucepan. Serve with the meatloaf.

MAKES 2 CUPS

chicken pot pies

ROUX
2 tablespoons butter
½ cup flour
½ cup Marsala wine

FILLING
½ cup flour
1 leaf fresh sage, minced
½ teaspoon nutmeg
½ teaspoon salt
½ teaspoon pepper
4 cups raw chicken breast, skinless, boneless and cubed in ½-inch pieces
2 tablespoons butter
¼ cup oil
½ cup pearl onions
2 cups heavy cream
2 cups milk
⅛ cup chicken base
(see Resources)
1 cup carrots, diced
1½ cups frozen green peas

Remove puff pastry from freezer and put in the refrigerator until ready to use. Prepare the roux by melting the butter in a saucepan. Stir in the flour and cook for 1 minute until mixture is bubbly. Add wine and return the mixture to boiling. Cook for 1 minute more, remove from heat and set aside.

For the filling, combine flour, nutmeg, fresh sage, salt and pepper; toss chicken in the flour mixture. Melt the butter and oil in a large a pan. Add chicken and sauté until golden brown. Remove chicken and set aside.

Sauté onions in the same pan and, when slightly browned, remove and set aside with the chicken.

Add the roux to pan and then stir in cream, milk and chicken base. Bring to a boil, stirring frequently to prevent lumps. If mixture gets too thick, thin with milk.

Add the chicken, onions and carrots to the sauce and continue cooking until the carrots are tender. Turn off heat and add the green peas.

To assemble the pies, preheat the oven to 425°F. Spray the inside of your ovenproof serving bowls with vegetable spray, being careful not to spray the edges. Fill bowls almost to the top with chicken and vegetable mixture.

(continued)

1 package frozen puff pastry sheets, thawed

1 egg

1 tablespoon milk

Pastry

Lay out the pastry sheets and divide into 6 pieces. Lightly roll the dough evenly in all four directions to extend it so it will completely cover the serving bowls. Cut a decorative ½-inch hole in the center of each piece to let steam escape and prevent it from getting soggy.

Put dough in the freezer for 10 minutes to chill, then remove and immediately lay the pastry over the tops of the bowls, pinching slightly to adhere. Trim around the edges with a knife, leaving a 1-inch edge. Make an egg wash with egg and milk, and brush the top of each pastry.

Put the bowls in the oven with a cookie sheet on the bottom shelf to catch any drips. Bake until the pastry is a medium-dark golden brown, about 20 to 30 minutes. Remove from oven and let set for 5 minutes and serve.

MAKES 6 SMALL PIES

jamaican pork tenderloin

With Sweet Potatoes and Mango Salsa

Pork must be brined at least 24 hours before preparing this dish

½ cup Mango Salsa
(see next page)

1½ pounds pork tenderloin, brined
(see next page)

½ cup butter

2 large sweet potatoes, cooked and sliced into rounds

pinch each salt, sugar and pepper

1 cup oil for frying bananas

2 bananas, peeled and sliced

½ cup all-purpose flour

½ cup peanuts, toasted
(optional)

Prepare Mango Salsa. Slice brined pork into six 4-ounce portions. Grill to medium temperature, 150-155°F on a meat thermometer; let rest and cut each portion into slices.

Melt butter in a hot frying pan. When butter is slightly browned, add sliced potatoes, a pinch each of salt, sugar and pepper. Cook potatoes until slightly caramelized.

Add oil to another large frying pan on high heat. While the oil is heating, toss sliced bananas with flour to coat. Fry sliced bananas in hot oil until golden brown. Remove from oil and drain on paper towels.

To serve, arrange sweet potatoes in the middle of the plate and fan out sliced pork next to them. Top with Mango Salsa, fried bananas and toasted peanuts.

MAKES 4 SERVINGS

BRINE

1½ cups water

⅓ cup plus 1 tablespoon sugar

⅛ cup salt

½ teaspoon red pepper
flakes, crushed

1½ teaspoons black
peppercorns

1½ teaspoons whole fennel seed

1 teaspoon dried thyme leaves

1 cup apple juice concentrate

½ tablespoon Chinese
five-spice powder

½ tablespoon cinnamon

SALSA

1 ripe mango, peeled, pitted
and diced (about 1½ cups)

½ medium red onion, diced

1 jalapeño, seeded and minced

1 small cucumber, diced
(about 1 cup)

½ cup red bell pepper, diced

3 tablespoons fresh cilantro
leaves, chopped

3 tablespoons fresh lime juice

3 tablespoons
sweet Thai chili sauce
(see Resources)

PORK BRINE

Mix all ingredients together. Put tenderloin into a
non-reactive container or plastic bag and pour the brine
mixture over the meat. Brine for 24 to 96 hours in
refrigerator.

MAKES 3 CUPS

MANGO SALSA

Combine all of the ingredients in a bowl and season to
taste with salt and pepper.

MAKES 2 CUPS

monkfish thermidor

2 pounds monkfish, skinned, cleaned and cubed

4 cups dry white wine

½ cup shallots, diced

2 cloves garlic, diced

½ cup seafood base
(see Resources)

2 sprigs fresh tarragon or 1 teaspoon dry

2 sprigs fresh parsley or 1 teaspoon dry

2 bay leaves

¼ pound butter (one stick)

1½ cups mushrooms, sliced

½ cup cognac or brandy

3 tablespoons flour

1 tablespoon cornstarch

2 cups heavy cream

¼ teaspoon ground nutmeg

1 tablespoon dry English mustard (or to taste)

1 cup Parmesan cheese

½ cup Gruyère cheese

fresh tarragon for garnish

This is one of my comfy, yummy, favorite winter seafood recipes and it's so easy. You can use any type of fish. I like to use monkfish, as its nickname "the poor man's lobster," says it all. It is a sweet, succulent and firm white fish that poaches extremely well. It is not cheap, but still less expensive than lobster.'

Clean and cube fish. Put wine, shallots, garlic, seafood base and herbs in a large pot and bring to a boil. Add monkfish and lower heat, simmering for about 20 minutes until the fish is opaque and cooked through. Remove fish with a slotted spoon and strain the liquid. Put liquid into large saucepan, bring to a boil and reduce by half. Set aside the fish and the reduced broth.

Melt butter in large skillet and sauté the mushrooms until golden brown. Add the cognac to deglaze the pan. Mix together the flour and cornstarch and slowly stir into the melted butter, cognac and mushrooms. Continue to cook until the mixture is bubbly, then slowly add the cream, stirring constantly.

Add the reduced fish broth and the cooked fish, nutmeg and mustard. Bring to boil and turn off heat. Mix in the cheeses, stirring until smooth. Taste and add more tarragon, mustard, salt and fresh ground pepper if needed. Ladle over rice and garnish with fresh tarragon. Serve with French bread and butter, a fresh herb salad and a crisp pinot grigio like Santa Margherita, or even a cold glass of milk!

scallop meyer lemon risotto

30 scallops, chemical-free or dry-packed, size 10-20

1 cup olive oil

3 tablespoons garlic, minced

2 tablespoons seafood base
(see Resources)

⅛ cup Perfect Puree Meyer Lemon Concentrate
(see Resources)

2 cups dry white wine

3 tablespoons garlic, minced

6 cups risotto, cooked

2 tablespoons capers

GARNISH

fresh-grated Parmesan cheese

2 tablespoons fresh parsley or fresh thyme, minced

paprika

lemon wedges

RISOTTO

4½ cups chicken or vegetable broth

1 cup dry white wine

1½ tablespoons olive oil

6 tablespoons butter

1½ cups Arborio rice

salt and fresh-ground black pepper

Pat scallops dry with paper towels. Heat half the oil in a large skillet until very hot; add half the scallops and cook for about one minute. Do not stir or move the scallops until they are golden brown. Turn to brown the other side for 1 to 2 minutes. Do not overcook. Drain on paper towels, then put scallops on a cookie sheet in a 200°F oven to keep warm. Add remaining oil to the pan and cook the rest of the scallops. Mix seafood base with wine and use this liquid to deglaze the skillet, scraping up browned bits, and bring to a boil. Let it boil until it reduces by a quarter, 5-8 minutes. Add cooked risotto and capers, stirring until hot and creamy.

Spoon risotto and sauce into warmed bowls, top with scallops, freshly grated Parmesan cheese and fresh parsley or thyme. Sprinkle with paprika and serve with lemon wedges.

MAKES 6 SERVINGS

RISOTTO

Bring broth and wine to a simmer in a medium saucepan. Using a heavy saucepan or Dutch oven, heat the oil and butter; add the rice and stir to coat. Add ½ cup of the simmering broth and stir constantly to keep the rice from sticking. When the broth is absorbed add the next ½ cup of broth. Continue this process until all the broth is absorbed; it takes about 20 minutes. The rice should be cooked al dente. Season to taste with salt and pepper.

MAKES 6 CUPS

BBQ big-ass shrimp

With Maque Choux

¼ pound butter

½ cup yellow onions, chopped

4 cloves garlic, minced

1 cup tomatoes, diced

1 teaspoon each fresh thyme, rosemary and parsley, minced

1 teaspoon Creole or Cajun seasoning
(see Resources)

1 lemon, zested and juiced

½ teaspoon black pepper

½ cup dark beer

1 teaspoon Worcestershire sauce

1 tablespoon Pickapeppa Sauce
(see Resources)

4 strips of smoked bacon, chopped

18 jumbo heads-on shrimp (size U-10) peeled and deveined

4 cups rice, cooked

They are not grilled and there is no BBQ sauce!

Prepare rice and set aside. To make the sauce, melt butter in a skillet on medium-high heat. Add the onions and sauté until clear; add garlic and cook until soft. Next, add all the remaining ingredients, except bacon, shrimp and rice, and bring to a boil. Cook at low boil for 10 minutes. Turn off heat and set aside.

Make the Maque Choux recipe on the next page and set aside. Fry the chopped bacon in a large sauté pan until the fat has rendered and the bacon is crispy. Add shrimp to pan with bacon fat and bacon pieces and sauté until the shrimp starts to turn pink; add the sauce and heat until sauce is hot. The shrimp will be fully cooked when the sauce is hot. Turn off heat and serve immediately.

Have 6 wide-rimmed bowls ready. Place a scoop of rice in each bowl and top with the sauce and equal amounts of shrimp. Serve with crisp, hot bread and butter, Maque Choux, Louisiana hot sauce and cold, dark beer.

This dish is simple: just huge, whole shrimp in lots of butter and black pepper. The essential ingredient is large, heads-on shrimp, since the fat in the shrimp heads makes most of the flavor.

MAKES 6 SERVINGS

2 tablespoons butter

3 cups corn, about 5 ears

1 cup yellow onions, chopped

1 cup green bell pepper, chopped

1 jalapeño, seeded and minced

1 teaspoon salt

1 teaspoon sweet paprika

½ cup tomatoes, diced

1 teaspoon fresh thyme, minced

½ cup heavy cream

salt and pepper to taste

MAQUE CHOUX

Melt butter in a skillet on medium-high heat. Add corn, onion, green pepper and jalapeño, salt and paprika. Cook until soft about 10 minutes. Add tomatoes, thyme and cream, and cook 2 minutes more. Remove from heat and serve.

MAKES 6 SERVINGS

BBQ Big-Ass Shrimp was created in the mid-1950s at Pascal's Manale Restaurant, an old family-run Italian-Creole restaurant located in uptown New Orleans that's famous for barbecued shrimp. A regular customer reported that he'd enjoyed a dish in a Chicago restaurant that he thought was made with shrimp, butter and pepper, and he asked Pascal Radosta to try and recreate it. Tasting Pascal's attempt, the customer said it was not quite the same, but he liked this new dish even better. Thus, the signature dish at Manale's Restaurant was born.

taos tamale pie

3 cups Lesley's
Frijoles Negros
(see page 213)

4 green chile
cheese tamales
(see Resources)

3 cups cooked,
chopped chicken

3 cups green or red New
Mexican chile sauce
(see page 202)

1 cup shredded Monterey
Jack or Cheddar cheese

GARNISH

2 cups shredded lettuce

⅓ cup each cooked corn,
julienned carrots
and julienned radishes

1 tomato, diced

2 avocados, sliced

¼ cup Cotija cheese

Preheat oven to 350°F. Prepare Lesley's Frijoles Negros and layer them in the bottom of an ovenproof serving dish.

Top with tamales, chicken, and red or green chile sauce. Bake in preheated oven for 30-40 minutes. Remove from oven and top with Jack or Cheddar cheese.

Garnish with veggies, sliced avocado and Cotija cheese.

Makes 4 servings

roast duck leg

With Lychee Coconut Sauce

1 tablespoon
coriander seeds

1 teaspoon fennel seeds

1 teaspoon cumin seeds

½ teaspoon whole black
peppercorns

4 teaspoons coarse
kosher salt

10 whole duck
leg/thigh pieces

2 cups olive oil

1 cup sake

2 cups chicken broth

2 medium onions, halved

6 cloves garlic

2 large lemons,
zested and juiced

2 tablespoons
red curry powder

1 tablespoon Chinese
five-spice powder

¼ cup fresh ginger, julienned
(no need to peel)

Toast first 4 ingredients in a skillet over medium heat until fragrant, about 2 minutes. Put toasted seeds in a mortar or spice grinder and grind to a coarse powder. Transfer to small bowl and stir in salt.

Arrange duck legs on a rimmed baking sheet and rub spice mixture over all sides. Refrigerate overnight. Do not cover; the duck legs need to be as dry as possible for sautéing.

When ready to cook, preheat oven to 300°F. Cook the duck in 2 batches. Heat 1 cup of olive oil in a large skillet over medium-high heat and cook duck, skin side down, until skin is crisp and brown, about 7 minutes; turn and cook until the other side is brown, about 3 minutes longer. Drain fat from skillet and cook second batch with 1 cup of fresh oil. When all the duck legs are browned, put them into a roasting pan, skin side up.

Pour off any remaining fat from skillet and add sake. Bring to a boil over medium-high heat, scraping up browned bits. Add chicken broth and boil until liquid is reduced by one-third. Pour mixture over the duck in the roasting pan.

Place onions, garlic, lemon zest and juice, spices and ginger around the meat and cover with foil. Cook duck in the oven for 30 minutes. Remove and turn legs over; cover again and cook until duck is tender and meat is falling off the bones, about 30 minutes more.

(continued)

SAUCE

**1 cup Perfect Puree
lychee fruit**
(see Resources)
or fresh lychee pureed

1 cup coconut milk

¼ cup cream of coconut

¼ cup sake

1 tablespoon cornstarch

1 tablespoon chicken base
(see Resources)

pinch garam masala
(see Resources or page 198)

Remove duck from the oven; take off the foil and let cool uncovered for 30 minutes. After duck has cooled, proceed with the next step or cover and refrigerate for up to 5 days.

For the final preparation, if duck has been refrigerated, let it come to room temperature. Brush meat with a little olive oil and put under the broiler, skin side up, at least 5 inches from the heat. Broil until the skin turns crisp and brown, about 4 minutes. Watch carefully to prevent burning.

Serve on rice or grilled sweet potatoes with Lychee Coconut Sauce.

MAKES 10 SERVINGS

LYCHEE COCONUT SAUCE

Mix all ingredients in a blender, then pour into a saucepan and bring to a boil. Cook for 2-3 minutes to thicken sauce. Cool and serve over the duck legs.

MAKES 2½ CUPS

sage brown butter chicken

6 Yukon gold potatoes

4 boneless chicken breasts, with skin

2 teaspoons each salt and pepper

¼ teaspoon ground nutmeg

½ cup bacon fat or olive oil
(I love bacon fat for the flavor and it does not burn at high temperatures)

Sage Brown Butter

BUTTER

½ pound butter (2 sticks), cut up

¼ cup fresh sage leaves plus extra for garnish

Preheat oven to 350°F. Scrub potatoes, pierce with a fork, and bake for about 35 minutes until al dente soft, not mushy but not hard. When done remove potatoes from the oven and leave the oven on. Cool potatoes and cut into ¼-inch-thick slices. Lay the potato slices in a baking dish and drizzle with a little olive oil. Using a clean surface, liberally salt, pepper and nutmeg the chicken breasts on the skinless side. Heat a large ovenproof skillet with oil or bacon fat until sizzling. Put the chicken in the pan skin side down and sear until brown. Turn chicken and brown the other side.

When chicken is brown on both sides, put the skillet in the oven, alongside the dish of potatoes, and cook for 15-20 minutes. The chicken is done when it registers 165°F on a meat thermometer. Do not to overcook or the chicken will be dry. While the chicken and potatoes are baking, make the Sage Brown Butter. Have 4 warmed plates ready. Divide the potatoes and layer on the plate. Top with the chicken, skin side up and drizzle with Sage Brown Butter. Finish with some fresh-ground pepper and paprika; garnish with fresh sage leaves.

MAKES 4 SERVINGS

SAGE BROWN BUTTER
Melt the butter in a sauté pan; add sage leaves and sauté until golden brown and the sage smells nutty.

MAKES 1 CUP

pollo borracho

1 (4-pound) frying chicken, cut into 8 pieces

1 teaspoon salt

½ teaspoon pepper

½ teaspoon granulated sugar

1 teaspoon ground cumin

1 teaspoon New Mexican red chile powder
(see Resources)

1 teaspoon dried Mexican oregano
(see Resources)

½ cup extra virgin olive oil

1 large onion, sliced thick

3 cloves garlic, chopped

1 bay leaf

½ cup dry white wine

1 cup tequila

1 cup tomatoes, diced

1 cup green chile, chopped

1 cup small to medium Spanish olives with pimientos, drained

2 cups white rice

fresh cilantro, chopped

Preheat oven to 375°F. Season chicken with salt, pepper, sugar, cumin, chile powder and oregano. In an ovenproof skillet or Dutch oven, heat olive oil and brown chicken pieces on all sides. Remove chicken from pan and set aside.

Reduce heat, add onion and garlic and cook for 5 minutes. Add the bay leaf, wine and tequila. Return chicken to the pan, cover, and bake in the oven for 30 minutes. Remove cover and add tomatoes, chopped chile and green olives. Return to the oven, uncovered, for another 10 to 15 minutes.

While chicken bakes, prepare the white rice. Stir chopped cilantro into the cooked, drained rice while it is still warm just before serving.

MAKES 4 SERVINGS

scallops moqueca

2 tablespoons each parsley and cilantro, minced

1 teaspoon mint, minced

4 jalapeños, seeded and cut into thin strips

1 onion, diced

3 cups tomatoes, diced with juice

⅛ cup garlic, chopped

1 teaspoon salt

2 tablespoons paprika

2 tablespoons cumin

1 cup dendê oil
(see Resources)

1 cup coconut milk

1 lime, zested and juiced

½ cup dark rum

½ cup seafood base
(see Resources)

⅓ cup cornstarch

2-3 tablespoons water

1½ pounds scallops, 10-20 size

3 cups rice, cooked

⅛ cup fresh cilantro, chopped

You will need dendê oil for the sauce and to sauté the scallops. Dendê oil (see Resources) *is a heavy tropical oil extracted from the African oil palm grown in northern Brazil. It adds a wonderful flavor and bright orange color to foods. If unavailable, you can get by with achiote paste pureed with one cup of olive oil.*

Combine parsley, cilantro, mint, jalapeños, onion and tomatoes; set aside. Chop garlic, put into a mortar with salt, paprika and cumin and mash into a paste. Heat a large pot on medium heat; add ⅓ cup of the oil. When the oil is hot, sauté garlic mixture lightly, add the tomato mixture, cooking until heated through. Next add the coconut milk, lime juice and zest, rum and seafood base.

Make a slurry with cornstarch and a little water, stirring until you get a paste. Add to the sauce, whisking, and bring to a boil. Cook for 1 minute and remove from heat. Sauce can be used immediately or refrigerated for up to 1 week; tightly covered and frozen, it will keep for 3 months.

Pat the scallops dry and season with salt and pepper. Heat ⅓ cup of the dendê oil in a large sauté pan until very hot. Add half of the scallops and sear. Do not stir or move the scallops until they are golden brown, then turn to brown the second side. This will take 1-2 minutes. Do not overcook. Remove scallops from the pan and drain on paper towels. Repeat with the remaining oil and scallops. Scoop rice into serving bowls, top with sauce and scallops, and garnish with chopped cilantro.

MAKES 6 SERVINGS

tequila lime shrimp

2 cups Tequila Lime Sauce

1½ pounds pasta,
cooked al dente

24 to 30 large raw shrimp,
peeled and deveined

1 red bell pepper, julienned

2-3 jalapeño peppers,
seeded and julienned

½ cup olive oil

½ teaspoon each
salt and pepper

2 tablespoons garlic, minced

GARNISH

Cotija or Parmesan
cheese, grated

fresh cilantro

SAUCE

1 cup margarita mix

¾ cup gold tequila

2 fresh limes,
zested and juiced

5 tablespoons
powdered sugar

¼ teaspoon salt

1 tablespoon cornstarch

Prepare Tequila Lime Sauce, cook pasta and set both aside. Peel and devein shrimp and prepare vegetables.

Heat oil in a large pan. When hot add shrimp, salt and pepper. Sauté shrimp until they start to turn pink. Immediately add garlic and peppers and sauté until garlic is opaque. Add the Tequila Lime Sauce, bring to quick boil and serve immediately with the pasta.

Garnish with Cotija or Parmesan cheese and fresh cilantro.

MAKES 6 SERVINGS

TEQUILA LIME SAUCE
Put liquids into a non-reactive saucepan. Mix together sugar, salt and cornstarch, and add to the pan. Bring to a boil, whisking well until mixture has thickened. Taste for salt or sugar and add more if needed.

MAKES 2 CUPS

tuscan—style rib eye

With Gorgonzola Polenta

4 (6-ounce) boneless
rib eye steaks

4 large portobello
mushrooms

1 head radicchio,
cut into 4 wedges

STEAK MARINADE

⅛ cup rosemary leaves,
packed tight

⅛ cup basil leaves,
packed tight

½ cup extra virgin olive oil

2 tablespoons balsamic
vinegar

2 small cloves garlic,
crushed

1 teaspoon kosher salt

1 teaspoon fresh-
ground pepper

VEGETABLE MARINADE

1 cup extra virgin olive oil

¼ cup balsamic vinegar

salt and pepper to taste

STEAK MARINADE

In a blender, combine the ingredients for the steak marinade and puree until smooth. Pour the mixture into a wide, shallow dish. Add steaks, turning to coat with marinade, cover and refrigerate for 2 hours or overnight.

VEGETABLE MARINADE

Combine ingredients in a wide shallow dish. Add portobellos and radicchio; marinate for 30 minutes.

Fire up the grill. While the grill is heating, make the Gorgonzola Polenta.

Put the steaks on the grill and cook, turning once, for about 6 to 9 minutes per side, or until desired doneness. Let the meat rest while grilling the vegetables. Put mushrooms and radicchio on the grill and cook until smoky and slightly soft. When done, remove from the grill and cut the portobellos into thick slices.

MAKES 4 SERVINGS

(continued)

2 cups chicken broth
(at room temperature)

2 cups milk
(at room temperature)

**1 cup polenta or
coarse-ground cornmeal**

**3 tablespoons
unsalted butter**

½ teaspoon nutmeg

zest of ½ lemon

½ cup Gorgonzola cheese

salt and pepper to taste

GORGONZOLA POLENTA

Put broth and milk into a large saucepan over medium heat. Gradually whisk in the polenta and bring to a boil, stirring constantly. Turn heat to low and cook until the mixture thickens and the cornmeal is tender, stirring often. Turn off the heat and add the butter, nutmeg, lemon zest and Gorgonzola, stirring until melted and blended. Season to taste with salt and pepper.

If you are in a hurry, pre-made polenta can be purchased in a tube at your supermarket. Heat the polenta, then add the butter, nutmeg, lemon zest and Gorgonzola, stirring to combine. Whole Foods, Trader Joe's and Costco or any Italian grocer carry the best brands. For gluten free use Ancient Harvest Quinoa Polenta *(see Resources)*.

Have 4 large plates ready. Put a scoop of polenta in the middle of the plate. Cut the steak against the grain into one-half-inch slices and fan them out on the polenta. Put the sliced portobellos on top of the steak. Serve with a wedge of grilled radicchio.

Pass the fresh ground pepper, crumbled Gorgonzola, balsamic vinegar and extra virgin olive oil.

MAKES 5 CUPS

sitivani's fijian shrimp

1 recipe Fijian Sauce

4 cups cooked
rice or noodles

1 recipe Spicy Shrimp

SAUCE

1 cup canola oil

2 tablespoons sesame oil

½ cup yellow onion, diced

1 tablespoon fresh ginger,
cut into matchsticks

2 tablespoons
garlic, minced

1 tablespoon soy sauce

1 lime, zested and juiced

1 tablespoon dark
brown sugar

2 teaspoons fish base
(see Resources)

1 can (14-ounce)
coconut milk

2 cans (14-ounce)
tomatoes, diced with juice

1 teaspoon ground pepper

½ teaspoon salt

When I worked in the Sinai, I hung out with the Fijians, whom I love. We drank kava, sang songs, had parties, and traveled throughout Egypt and Israel. Lt. Colonel Sitivani (Steve) Rabuka threw me a big party for my birthday and made this dish. It can be served with rice or noodles.

Gather all ingredients and have them ready to cook. Prepare sauce and rice or noodles and keep them warm. Prepare the garnishes and set aside. When ready to serve, cook the spicy shrimp and serve immediately.

FIJIAN SAUCE

Put the canola and sesame oil in a large saucepan and heat. Add onion and cook until glassy, then add ginger and garlic and stir for about 1 minute until soft. Be very careful not to burn the garlic. Add soy sauce, lime zest, lime juice, sugar, fish base, coconut milk, tomatoes, pepper and salt. Bring to a boil, remove from heat and set aside.

MAKES 4 CUPS

(continued)

1 cup canola oil

2 tablespoons sesame oil

1½ pounds shrimp,
peeled and deveined

pinch each salt and pepper

¼ teaspoon ground coriander

4 jalapeños,
seeded and julienned

4 cups Fijian Sauce

4 large fresh basil leaves

2 cups fresh spinach

GARNISH

2 jalapeños,
veins and seeds
removed, chopped

2-inch knob fresh ginger,
peeled, slivered and fried

Hot sauce to taste

Spicy Shrimp

Have servings bowls and rice or noodles ready. Heat the canola and sesame oils in a large sauté pan, making sure it's big enough to hold the sauce and shrimp. Lightly salt and pepper the shrimp and put them in the hot oil.

Add the coriander and cook the shrimp until pink and opaque. Add jalapeños, stir for 30 seconds and then add the Fijian Sauce.

Add the basil and spinach last, stirring into the hot sauce so they wilt. Taste and adjust with salt, pepper or sugar, adding a little at a time.

Ladle the shrimp and sauce over rice or noodles, dividing shrimp into equal servings. Garnish with the jalapeños and fresh ginger, and pass the hot sauce of your choice.

Makes 4 to 6 servings

tuxedo sesame tuna

With Five-Spice Risotto and Wasabi Cream

4 (6-ounce) fresh tuna steaks

1 tablespoon fresh lime zest

¼ teaspoon salt

½ to 1 teaspoon coarse-ground black pepper

¼ cup of black and white (tuxedo) sesame seeds
(see Resources)

2 tablespoons olive oil

2 tablespoons sesame oil

4 cups Five-Spice Risotto

1 cup Wasabi Cream
(see next page)

nori for garnish
(see Resources)

RISOTTO

3 cups chicken or vegetable broth

⅔ cup dry white wine

1 tablespoon olive oil

4 tablespoons butter

1 cup Arborio rice

¼ teaspoon Chinese five-spice powder
(see Resources)

salt and fresh-ground black pepper

Prepare Five-Spice Risotto, cover and set aside. Prepare the Wasabi Cream. Sprinkle lime zest, salt and pepper on the top of the tuna steaks. Press the bottom of each steak into the black and white sesame seeds, coating them well.

Put olive and sesame oil in a heavy-bottomed sauté pan or skillet on high heat. Put tuna into the pan, sesame side down, searing for 1 minute. Turn the steaks over carefully, reducing the heat to medium, and sear the other side for 1 more minute, cooking until medium rare. Do not overcook the tuna or it will become dry and lose its flavor.

To serve, put a scoop of cooked risotto in the middle of a plate, cut tuna in half on the bias so it is angled. Stack tuna at an angle on the risotto and pour ¼ cup Wasabi Cream over the tuna. Garnish with nori *(see Resources)*.

MAKES 4 SERVINGS

FIVE-SPICE RISOTTO

Bring broth and wine to simmer in a saucepan. Using a large saucepan or Dutch oven, heat the oil and butter. Add rice and stir to coat. Add ½ cup of the simmering broth to the rice, stirring to keep the rice from sticking. When the broth is absorbed, add the next ½ cup. Repeat, stirring constantly, until all the broth is absorbed, about 20 minutes. Mix in the five-spice powder and season to taste with salt and pepper.

MAKES 4 CUPS

1 cup heavy cream

2 tablespoons
sour cream

½ teaspoon wasabi powder
or paste, to taste

1 teaspoon cornstarch

WASABI CREAM

Mix together the heavy cream and sour cream. Add ½ teaspoon wasabi powder or paste to the cream mixture and taste until you have the intensity you want; a little goes a long way. Start with ½ teaspoon and work your way up.

Pour the cream mixture into a small saucepan and heat. If the sauce needs to be thickened, use a small amount of cornstarch mixed with a little water to make a paste. Blend in the cornstarch paste and cook for at least a minute. Serve warm.

MAKES 1 CUP

pappardelle with spinach

And Mushrooms in Goat Cheese Sauce

1 pound Italian pappardelle, cooked al dente

¼ cup extra virgin olive oil

2 cups button mushrooms, halved

2 tablespoons onion, minced

1 tablespoon garlic, minced

½ cup dry white wine

1 cup goat cheese

2 cups heavy cream

2 tablespoons basil, minced

2 tablespoons parsley, minced

1 teaspoon thyme, minced

1 teaspoon lemon zest

salt and pepper to taste

4 cups loose baby spinach

Cook pappardelle al dente and drain; do not rinse. Mix noodles with a little olive oil so they don't congeal; set aside. Heat 2 tablespoons of olive oil in a large sauté pan and, when hot, add half of the mushrooms. Do not crowd the pan. When they are cooked to a golden brown, remove from the pan and set aside. Add 2 more tablespoons of oil and, when hot, add the remaining mushrooms. Cook until golden brown, remove from pan and set aside.

Add onions to the pan and sauté for 1 minute; add garlic and sauté until garlic is soft and translucent, about 45 seconds. Always add garlic after the onions because onions take longer to cook and garlic burns easily.

Add wine to deglaze the pan, cooking for a minute longer and then add the goat cheese and cream. Mix well and cook until the goat cheese is melted and smooth and the sauce is hot.

Add the herbs, lemon zest, salt and pepper. Remove from heat. Mix the cooked pappardelle, spinach and mushrooms in the sauce to heat through and serve immediately.

MAKES 4 SERVINGS

T-bone for two

With Wild Porcinis and Chanterelles

STEAK

24-ounce T-Bone steak
(at room temperature)

2 tablespoons olive oil

2 teaspoons kosher salt

**1 tablespoon cracked
black pepper**

**1 sprig fresh rosemary,
off the stem and chopped**

SAUCE

2 tablespoons olive oil

1 tablespoon butter

**¾ cup porcini mushrooms,
sliced thick**

**1¾ cup chanterelles,
cut in half**

1 small shallot, chopped

2 cloves garlic, chopped

½ cup merlot wine

**1 tablespoon fresh
thyme, chopped**

**1 tablespoon flat-leaf
parsley, chopped**

1 tablespoon cold butter

**fresh-ground black
pepper to taste**

Rub the steak with the olive oil, salt, pepper and fresh chopped rosemary. Set aside until ready to grill. Heat the grill to moderate heat, making sure the grill is clean and the rack has been oiled beforehand.

Grill steak 8 to 10 minutes per side for medium-rare. When done, allow the meat to rest for a few minutes before carving, and transfer to a warmed serving platter.

While the steak is grilling, assemble the ingredients for the sauce. Heat the oil in a large sauté pan.

When hot, add the butter, then add the mushrooms, giving them plenty of room to sauté. If the pan is too small and the mushrooms are crowded, sauté them in 2 batches, repeating the olive oil and butter.

Remove mushrooms from the pan and sauté the shallots and garlic. Add the merlot to deglaze the pan. Return mushrooms to the pan; add thyme and parsley to the sauce and bring to a boil.

Remove from the heat and stir in 1 tablespoon of cold butter and fresh-ground black pepper before serving.

If you cannot find porcini or chanterelle mushrooms, use criminis or portobellos, which are usually available in the produce section of your local supermarket.

MAKES 2 SERVINGS

chicken enchiladas

With Mango and Green Chile

¼ cup olive oil

1 small onion, diced

1 pound skinless, boneless chicken breasts and thighs

2 cups tomatoes, diced

2 teaspoons ground cumin

2 teaspoons dry oregano

2 cups chicken broth

2 cups mango puree
(see Resources)

2 cups New Mexican green chile sauce
(see page 202)

1 tablespoon Cholula hot sauce
(optional)

8 (7-inch) flour tortillas

1 pound Monterey Jack cheese, shredded

½ cup Cotija cheese, grated

¼ cup green onions, chopped

¼ cup black olives, chopped

¼ cup fresh cilantro, chopped

Heat the olive oil in a large pot and, when hot, add onion and sauté until soft. Add the chicken, tomatoes, cumin, oregano and broth. Cover and cook until chicken is very tender and can be pulled apart.

Remove chicken with a slotted spoon and let cool slightly, then shred with your hands and set aside. Return the tomato mixture to a boil and reduce the sauce down to one cup. Stir the mango puree and green chile sauce into the tomato mixture. For a spicier sauce, add 1 tablespoon Cholula or your favorite hot sauce.

Preheat oven to 350°F. Lightly grease a 9x14-inch baking dish and cover the bottom with a layer of sauce. Fill each tortilla with equal amounts of chicken and Monterey Jack cheese, reserving remaining cheese for topping. Roll tortillas to form enchiladas and arrange them in the baking dish. Cover the enchiladas with the remaining sauce and bake for 30 minutes. Top with Monterey Jack cheese and Cotija cheese, and continue baking for 5 minutes, until cheese is melted. Remove from the oven and top with green onions, black olives and cilantro.

Let set for 10 minutes before serving. Cut between every 2 enchiladas before serving, they will be easier to get out of the pan. Place 2 enchiladas on a large plate with Lesley's Frijoles Negros *(see page 213)*.

MAKES 4 SERVINGS

corned beef hash

4 medium potatoes, cooked and diced

5 cups (about 3 pounds) lean corned beef, cooked

2 tablespoons olive oil

2 onions, diced

1 tablespoon garlic, minced

2 tablespoons fresh thyme leaves, minced

½ cup fresh parsley, minced

pinch dry mustard

¼ teaspoon nutmeg

½ teaspoon fresh-ground pepper

¼ cup chicken broth

¼ cup dry white wine

½ cup Worcestershire sauce

salt to taste

Dice and cook potatoes until tender. Dice corned beef and place in a large bowl. Heat olive oil in a medium pan and sauté the onions until clear, then add garlic and turn off heat. Let onion and garlic cool, then add to corned beef. Add herbs and spices, chicken broth, wine, Worcestershire sauce and potatoes to corned beef, mixing well. Taste and season with salt, if needed.

To make the hash, heat a sauté pan with enough vegetable oil to cover the bottom. When the oil is hot, cook the hash until crispy on one side then flip the hash over to cook the other side. Serve with poached eggs or by itself for a simple dinner.

Delicious with New Mexican Green Chile Hollandaise Sauce *(see page 208)*.

MAKES 6 TO 8 SERVINGS

pumpkin ravioli

In Hazelnut Cream Sauce with Arugula

FILLING

½ cup unsalted butter

1 onion, diced

1 clove garlic, minced

2 teaspoons ground coriander seed

½ teaspoon each ground mace and ground allspice

1 pinch ground cardamom

2 teaspoons cumin

½ teaspoon cinnamon

3 tablespoons New Mexican red chile powder
(see Resources)

1 cup pumpkin puree

⅓ pound Parmesan cheese, grated

2 tablespoons real maple syrup

3 tablespoons brown sugar

1 egg, beaten

2 teaspoons salt

1 teaspoon ground black pepper

2½ pounds fresh pasta sheets
(see Resources or make your own, see right)

If you are making fresh pasta, do this first and put the dough in the refrigerator to chill while you prepare the filling and sauce.

FILLING

Melt butter in a skillet and sauté the onions, garlic and spices until the onions are soft. Add the pureed pumpkin cheese, maple syrup, brown sugar, egg, salt and black pepper. Taste to adjust seasonings and set the filling aside.

MAKES 2 CUPS

PASTA *(see right)*

Put all ingredients in food processor and pulse until dough pulls away from the sides of container and forms a ball. Knead 5-10 times on a surface that is lightly coated with the same flour used to make the dough.

Cover with a damp towel and let rest for 30 minutes.

When ready to use, roll dough out with a pasta roller, KitchenAid attachment or by hand. Just make sure that if you use a rolling pin, you roll evenly and get the dough as thin as possible.

MAKES 2½ POUNDS

(continued)

PASTA

4 cups semolina, bread flour or unbleached all-purpose flour

8 large eggs

1½ teaspoons salt

2 tablespoons extra virgin olive oil

SAUCE

1 cup hazelnuts, skinned and toasted

2 tablespoons butter

3 cups heavy whipping cream

3 cloves garlic, minced

pinch each cayenne and white pepper

pinch salt

2 cups arugula, plus 1 tablespoon, chopped

HAZELNUT CREAM SAUCE

Chop the hazelnuts coarsely, reserving ¼ cup for garnish. Melt the butter in a skillet, turn the heat to medium and add ¾ cup of chopped nuts. Cook the nuts, tossing frequently, until browned, 4-5 minutes. Add the cream, garlic, cayenne and white pepper to the nuts; turn heat to high and stir often. Do not let the cream boil over. When the cream is thick enough to coat the back of a spoon, add a pinch of salt, seasoning to taste. Set aside.

To make the ravioli, lay one sheet of pasta on a flat surface. Spray the dough with water to prevent drying and to make it more flexible. Put a heaping teaspoon of filling all along the bottom edge of the pasta sheet, about ½-inch apart. For larger ravioli, use a tablespoon of filling, leaving an inch between dollops. Fold the pasta sheet over the filling and cut the ravioli apart with a ravioli cutter. If you don't have a ravioli cutter, use a knife and seal the edges with the tines of a fork. Set the finished ravioli aside and cover with a damp cloth.

Bring a large pot of salted water to a boil. Cook the ravioli al dente and drain. To serve, arrange the arugula in bowls and place the ravioli on top, then pour the sauce over both. Garnish with remaining chopped hazelnuts and chopped arugula.

MAKES 6 SERVINGS

salmon el diablo

3 cups white rice, cooked

6 portions fresh salmon,
5-6 ounces each

¼ cup Savory Spice Mix
(see page 194)

SAUCE

¼ cup olive oil

1 shallot, diced

3 cloves garlic, crushed

2 cups crushed tomatilloes
*(see Tips, how to prepare
tomatilloes on page 219)*

¼ to ½ cup chipotle
in adobo sauce, pureed

½ cup green chile,
chopped

2 tablespoons orange zest

¼ cup capers

¼ cup Spanish olives, sliced

½ tablespoon salt

½ tablespoon pepper

½ tablespoon cumin

¼ cup cilantro leaves, minced

⅛ cup mint leaves, minced

2 tablespoons seafood base
(see Resources)

DIABLO SAUCE

Prepare rice and have all sauce ingredients prepped and ready to go. Heat olive oil in a large sauté pan. Add the shallots and sauté until clear then add garlic and sauté until soft. Add all remaining ingredients, bring to a boil and turn off the heat. Taste and adjust seasonings with salt and pepper and chipotle.

Fire up the grill and make sure it is clean, well oiled and ready for the salmon. Coat one side of the salmon with Savory Spice Mix and grill for 3 minutes, turn clockwise and cook for another 3 minutes.

Turn salmon over carefully and cook for an additional 5-6 minutes. Fish, like meat, will continue cooking when removed from the heat, so undercook slightly.

To serve, pour a large ladle of Diablo Sauce in the middle of each of 6 wide-rimmed bowls, add a rounded scoop of rice and stack the cooked salmon on top of the rice. Drizzle the Diablo Sauce over the middle of the salmon. Garnish with fresh cilantro sprigs and serve with crusty, hot bread and butter.

MAKES 6 SERVINGS

duck tagine

With Cauliflower Sauce and Couscous

4 duck breasts

¼ cup argan oil
(see Resources or use olive oil)

1 teaspoon ground coriander

1 teaspoon paprika

½ teaspoon turmeric

1 tablespoon ground cumin

¼ teaspoon ground nutmeg

salt and fresh-ground black pepper

This deconstructed dish contains all the classic components found in the "original." The difference is in the preparation. When creating a dish using deconstructive techniques, the ingredients are essentially prepared and treated on their own It is during the plating and presentation stages that everything is brought together.

DUCK

Preheat oven to 350°F. Score the skin of the duck breast with a sharp knife and then rub with a little argan oil. Mix together the ground coriander, paprika, turmeric, cumin and nutmeg and rub into the oiled duck breast. Season well with salt and fresh-ground black pepper.

Heat an ovenproof frying pan until smoking hot; add the remaining oil and fry the duck skin-side down for five minutes or until golden brown and slightly crisp. Turn the duck breast over (skin side up) and finish in the oven for 6-8 minutes, or until cooked through but still slightly pink in the middle. Remove from the heat, cover with foil and let rest.

(continued)

2 cups cauliflower florets

2 tablespoons argan oil
or olive oil

2 lemons,
zested and juiced

1 clove garlic, minced

1 red onion, diced

2 tablespoons fresh
ginger, julienned

1 teaspoon harissa
(see page 199)

1 teaspoon cumin
seeds, toasted

1 teaspoon coriander
seeds, toasted

1 teaspoon turmeric

1 teaspoon tomato paste

1 (16-ounce) can tomatoes,
chopped with juice

1 bay leaf

2 tablespoon fresh
mint, chopped

1 cup dried apricots,
julienned

MOROCCAN CAULIFLOWER TOMATO SAUCE

Preheat oven to 425°F. Put the cauliflower florets on a baking tray or cookie sheet, drizzle with 1 tablespoon argan oil and roast for about 12 minutes, turning once.

Using a blender or food processor, mix together the zest and juice of 1 lemon, garlic, onion, ginger and harissa. Heat 1 tablespoon of oil and cook this mixture gently for 10 minutes.

Grind the toasted cumin and coriander seeds to a powder and add along with the turmeric, tomato paste, chopped tomatoes and bay leaf. Continue cooking for 20 minutes, remove the bay leaf and season to taste. Set aside. Add the mint and apricots just before serving.

MAKES 5 CUPS

(Couscous and plating instructions next page.)

⅛ cup olive oil

4 cloves garlic, minced

1 tablespoon fresh
ginger, grated

½ teaspoon ground
nutmeg

¼ teaspoon ground
cinnamon

½ teaspoon
ground cumin

1 orange, zest only

pinch saffron

2 cups couscous

salt and fresh-
ground black pepper

½ cup zucchini, diced

½ cup red bell
pepper, diced

GARNISH
toasted almonds
sliced dried apricots
sliced preserved lemons
(see Resources)

COUSCOUS

Heat the olive oil, reserving 2 tablespoons, in a small pan; add the garlic and ginger and sauté for one minute. Add the nutmeg, cinnamon, cumin, orange zest, and saffron; fry for one minute. Add the couscous and stir well, pouring enough boiling water to cover the couscous by ½-inch. Cover and remove from the heat. Let sit for 2-3 minutes or until all the water has been absorbed and the couscous is tender. Drizzle with a little olive oil, season with salt and fresh-ground black pepper, and fluff up the couscous grains with a fork.

Dice the zucchini and red pepper. In a large skillet, add 1 tablespoon of olive oil and heat until very hot. Sauté the zucchini and red pepper for about 1 minute and mix into the cooked couscous.

MAKES 2 CUPS

To serve the Tagine, use 4 wide, shallow bowls and put one cup of the Cauliflower Tomato Sauce in each. Using a scoop or spoon, place a ½-cup mound of couscous in the middle of the sauce. Lay the sliced duck on top of the couscous and drizzle with more of the sauce. Garnish with toasted almonds, sliced dried apricots and sliced preserved lemons.

MAKES 4 SERVINGS

divine desserts

homemade donuts

½ cup lukewarm water

2¼ teaspoons dry yeast

1 can (14-ounce) sweetened condensed milk

¼ teaspoon salt

⅛ teaspoon nutmeg

¼ teaspoon cinnamon

¼ teaspoon almond extract

½ teaspoon vanilla extract

2 cups cake flour

1 tablespoon vegetable oil plus oil for frying

½ cup Cinnamon Sugar Mix (see below)

CINNAMON SUGAR MIX

Mix together

1 cup sugar

⅓ cup cinnamon

1 teaspoon Chinese five-spice powder (see Resources)

Pour warm water into the mixing bowl of a stand mixer. Sprinkle the yeast over the water and let dissolve for 5 minutes. Add the milk, salt, spices, and almond and vanilla extracts.

Using the dough-hook attachment, combine the ingredients on low speed. Add half the flour and continue to beat on low speed until incorporated. Add remaining flour and turn up the speed to medium. Beat until well combined, about 4 to 5 minutes, and the dough pulls away from the bowl and becomes smooth.

Transfer dough to a well-oiled bowl, and roll the dough around until it is completely coated in oil. Cover the bowl with a tea towel and let rise in a warm place for 1 to 2 hours, until it has doubled in size.

On a well-floured surface, roll out dough to ⅜ inches thick. Cut out doughnuts using a 1-inch-round pastry cutter. Set them on a floured baking sheet, cover lightly with a tea towel, and let rise until doubled in size, 30 minutes to an hour.

Preheat oil in a deep fryer or Dutch oven to 365°F. Gently drop the doughnuts into the oil, 3 or 4 at a time. Cook for 1 minute per side. Remove from hot oil and place on paper towels to drain. While they are hot, sprinkle liberally with Cinnamon Sugar Mix. Serve immediately.

MAKES 32 DONUTS

pumpkin cheesecake

With Gingersnap and Pecan Crust

CRUST

1½ cups gingersnap cookies, ground

1½ cups pecans, toasted (about 6 ounces)

¼ cup brown sugar, packed firm

¼ cup (½ stick) unsalted butter, melted

FILLING

4 (8-ounce) packages cream cheese *(at room temperature)*

1⅔ cups sugar

1½ cups canned solid-pack pumpkin

9 tablespoons whipping cream

1 teaspoon ground cinnamon

1 teaspoon ground allspice

4 large eggs

Preheat oven to 350°F. Finely grind cookies, pecans and sugar in food processor. Add melted butter and blend until combined. Press crust mixture into the bottom and up the sides of two 9-inch-diameter springform pans with 2¾-inch-high sides.

FILLING

Using an electric mixer, beat cream cheese and sugar in a large bowl until light. Transfer ¾ cup of the mixture to a small bowl; cover tightly and refrigerate to use later for topping. Add pumpkin, 4 tablespoons of the whipping cream, cinnamon and allspice to remaining mixture in the large bowl and beat until well combined.

Add eggs, one at a time, beating just until combined. Pour filling into crust (it will almost fill the pan). Bake until cheesecake puffs, top browns and center moves only slightly when pan is shaken, about 1¼ hours.

Transfer cheesecake to rack and cool 10 minutes. Run a small sharp knife around cake pan sides to loosen cheesecake. When completely cooled, cover tightly and refrigerate overnight. Bring reserved ¾ cup of cream-cheese mixture to room temperature. Add the remaining 5 tablespoons whipping cream to cream-cheese mixture and stir to combine. Pour cream-cheese mixture over cheesecake, spreading evenly.

MAKES TWO 9-INCH CHEESECAKES

strawberry rhubarb galette

PASTRY

1 batch Fail-Proof Pie Crust dough
(see page 162)

1 egg

½ cup milk

8 teaspoons granulated sugar

FILLING

3 cups rhubarb, cut into 1-inch pieces

3 cups strawberries, quartered

¼ cup cornstarch

1 cup granulated white sugar

large pinch cinnamon

small pinch ginger

My Father's Favorite

He would never have called it a "galette" (a free-form rustic tart) but I do.

FILLING

Combine filling ingredients, except rhubarb, in a large bowl. Put the rhubarb in a large sauté pan and cook, covered over low heat until tender, about 15 minutes. If it dries out, add 1 teaspoon water while cooking. Mix cooked rhubarb with the rest of the filling ingredients.

Follow instructions for Fail-Proof Pie Crust dough, but form pie dough into a ball and section into 8 wedges. Roll each wedge into 6-inch flat round discs, free form; no cutters or tart forms needed.

Divide the filling ingredients into eighths, and place a heap of filling in the middle of each dough section. Try to keep the filling in the middle. Now fold up the edges of the dough about 1 inch, overlapping and pleating around the filling. When you are finished, it will look like a little basket, with the dough framing the fruit.

Mix the egg and milk to make an egg wash and brush on the dough. Sprinkle each galette with sugar and chill for 30 minutes.

Preheat oven to 350°F and bake the galettes for 20 to 30 minutes, until the crust is dark golden brown. Let cool slightly and serve while hot with vanilla ice cream. The galettes can be reheated in the oven for 8 to 10 minutes or in the microwave for no more that 45 seconds.

MAKES 8 GALETTES

my mother's jellyroll

1 Basic Sponge Cake recipe
(see page 163)

½ cup powdered sugar

½ cup cornstarch

1½ cups preserves
(I like plum, but use your favorite)

Preheat oven to 325°F and line a 12x18-inch baking sheet with parchment paper. Lightly spray the parchment with vegetable oil. Prepare batter for the Basic Sponge Cake according to the recipe. Pour batter into the pan, level with a straight edge and knock it once on the countertop to remove the bigger bubbles.

Bake for 12-15 minutes with the oven light on so you can see the color and rise of cake. Do not open the oven door until you see that the cake is browning, but be careful not to overcook.

The sponge cake needs to be warm to make a roll. While batter is baking, set out a clean kitchen towel and mix the powdered sugar and cornstarch together in a strainer or sifter. When the cake is done, let set for 5 minutes, remove it from the pan and put it on the clean towel. Peel off the parchment paper and sprinkle the cake with powdered sugar-cornstarch mix. Roll up the cake gently, leaving the towel inside as you roll. Do not roll tightly like a sushi roll or the cake will tear. Leave the cake rolled up and let it cool for 30 minutes. This forms the cake roll and makes it easy to prepare the jellyroll later.

After 30 minutes, unroll the cake and remove the towel. Spread preserves evenly inside the cake and re-roll without the towel. Slice and serve at room temperature. A jellyroll can also be filled with ice cream or a whipped cream mousse.

Makes 8 servings

lemon pound cake

With Blueberry Compote

¾ **pound butter**
(at room temperature)

1 cup sugar

3 eggs

2 lemons, zested and juiced

¼ **cup sour cream**

1 tablespoon vanilla

1 cup flour

1 cup semolina

1 teaspoon salt

¼ **teaspoon nutmeg**

½ **teaspoon baking soda**

½ **teaspoon baking powder**

⅛ **teaspoon cream of tartar**

3 cups Blueberry Compote

Preheat oven to 350°F. Grease and dust a 9-inch spring-form pan with semolina. Cream butter in a mixer then add sugar and continue whipping until light in color. Add eggs one at a time, beating well after each addition until mixture becomes light and fluffy. Add lemon juice and zest, sour cream and vanilla. Keep whipping for another 2 minutes.

Mix together dry ingredients in a separate bowl. Slowly add to liquid mixture, folding in with a spoon. Do not overmix.

Pour cake into prepared pan and bake for about 30 minutes until top of cake is golden brown and a tooth-pick inserted in the center comes out clean.

MAKES ONE 9-INCH CAKE

COMPOTE

1 cup white sugar

3 tablespoons cornstarch

⅛ **teaspoon ground cinnamon**

pinch each nutmeg and salt

1 cup red wine or grape juice

¼ **cup water**

1 lemon, zested and juiced

2 cups blueberries

½ **teaspoon almond extract**

½ **teaspoon vanilla extract**

BLUEBERRY COMPOTE

In a small bowl, mix together sugar, cornstarch, cinnamon, nutmeg and salt. In a saucepan over medium heat, combine the wine, water, and lemon juice and zest. Stir gently and bring to a boil. Whisk the cornstarch mixture into the liquid. Bring back to a boil and simmer gently. Add the blueberries, cooking on a low boil for 5 minutes. Remove from heat and stir in the almond and vanilla extracts. If the sauce is too runny, cook longer. If it's too thick, add a little wine or juice.

MAKES 3 CUPS

fail-proof pie crust

Flaky and Delicious

3 cups all-purpose flour

1 teaspoon kosher salt

2 teaspoons granulated sugar

pinch baking powder

16 tablespoons cold unsalted butter (2 sticks), cut into small pieces

½ cup ice water, plus 1 to 2 tablespoons, if needed

Combine flour, salt, sugar and baking powder in a large bowl and stir briefly until mixture is aerated. Using a pastry blender or your fingers, cut butter into dry ingredients until the dough is in pea-size pieces, 4 to 5 minutes. The dough will be slightly yellow in color.

Drizzle in ice water and mix just until dough comes together. (Add another tablespoon of ice water if necessary, but do not overwork the dough or it will become tough). Shape dough into a flat disk, cover in plastic wrap, and refrigerate for at least 30 minutes, then use the dough in the pie or tart recipe of your choice.

For quicker prep, you can make this dough in a food processor. Put all dry ingredients in the processor and pulse to combine. Add butter and pulse until it is in pea-size pieces. Drizzle in 3 tablespoons ice water and pulse again. Add more ice water if the dough seems too dry. Shape into a disk, wrap and refrigerate.

MAKES TWO 9-INCH CRUSTS

basic sponge cake

1 cup cake flour, sifted

pinch each cream of tartar and salt

6 large eggs
(at room temperature)

1 cup extra-fine granulated sugar

1 tablespoon lemon juice

½ teaspoon lemon zest

Heat oven to 325°F. Spray a 10x15x1-inch sheet pan with vegetable spray and line with parchment paper. Sift cake flour, cream of tartar and salt together and set aside.

Separate the whites from the yolks of the eggs, making sure you do not get ANY yolk in the whites. *(See how to beat egg whites on page 220.)* Following those directions, beat the egg whites until they form medium-stiff peaks. Once the egg whites are done, remove from bowl.

Beat the egg yolks until they are thick and turn a lemony color. Add the sugar in small quantities, beating between each addition. Add lemon juice and lemon zest. Beat well.

In small batches, fold the flour mixture into egg-yolk mixture, then gently fold in the beaten egg whites. Spread batter evenly in the pan and put into the oven to bake for 12 to 15 minutes, until the cake puffs up, loses its shine, and springs back when gently pressed. Be careful not to overcook. Remove from the oven and let cool slightly. Invert pan, removing the cake and the paper.

This recipe is used in My Mother's Jellyroll recipe on page 159, and I support a culinary comeback for the classic jellyroll.

MAKES ONE CAKE

banana coconut cream pie

With Vanilla Wafer Coconut Crust

CRUST
30 vanilla wafers, crushed
½ cup coconut, toasted
1½ tablespoons sugar
¼ cup butter melted
1 teaspoon vanilla extract

FILLING
⅔ cup sugar
3 tablespoons cornstarch
½ teaspoon salt
3 cups coconut milk
3 egg yolks, slightly beaten
1 tablespoon butter
(at room temperature)
1½ teaspoons vanilla extract
**2 medium bananas,
ripe but not brown**
½ cup coconut, toasted

Preheat oven to 375°F. Lightly toast the coconut in a hot, dry skillet on top of the stove or on a cookie sheet in the oven for 5-10 minutes. Put vanilla wafers, toasted coconut and sugar in a food processor and finely grind. Melt butter, add vanilla extract and pour over the dry ingredients. Pulse until well blended. Press into an even layer against the bottom and sides of a 9-inch pie pan. Bake for 5 to 7 minutes, and let cool before filling.

FILLING

Mix sugar, cornstarch and salt in a saucepan. Gradually stir in coconut milk. Cook over medium heat, stirring constantly until mixture thickens. Boil 1 minute more, stirring constantly, and remove from heat.

Whisk egg yolks and gradually stir ⅓ of the hot coconut milk mixture into the egg yolks, whisking constantly. Then pour this egg mixture back into the saucepan with the rest of the hot milk mix. Boil for 3-5 minutes, stirring constantly as the sauce thickens. Remove from heat and blend in butter and vanilla.

Peel and slice bananas and lay them in the finished piecrust. Immediately pour the filling over the bananas. Fill the pie shell halfway and sprinkle toasted coconut over filling. Finish filling pie shell with the rest of the filling, and cool to room temperature. Serve with fresh whipped cream and toasted coconut or Caramelized Pineapple Sauce.

MAKES ONE 9-INCH PIE

caramelized pineapple sauce

SAUCE

1 small pineapple

¼ cup butter, melted
*(if using unsalted butter
add a pinch of salt)*

**¼ cup dark brown sugar,
packed firm**

2 tablespoons dark rum

**2 tablespoons
pure vanilla extract**

Peel and core the pineapple, removing any brown dimples, and chop into small dice.

Melt the butter, brown sugar, rum and vanilla in a large sauté pan and add the pineapple cubes. Cook over low-medium heat for about 10 minutes, until the sugar has caramelized. Remove from heat and let cool, then put in a blender and puree.

MAKES 2 CUPS

s'mores chocolate nachos

**6-8 large flour tortillas,
cut into wedges**

**1 cup canola oil
for frying**

**1 tablespoon
ground cinnamon**

½ cup granulated sugar

**½ cup semisweet
chocolate chips**

**½ cup white
chocolate chips**

2 cups mini marshmallows
(or make your own, see page 187)

**chocolate and caramel
syrups in squeeze bottles**

fresh strawberries

**vanilla or chocolate
ice cream**

Fry tortilla wedges in hot canola oil until crisp. Remove from oil and immediately sprinkle with cinnamon and sugar; set aside.

When ready to make nachos, preheat oven to 350°F. Put tortilla wedges on an ovenproof plate and cover with chocolate chips and marshmallows. You can also substitute peanut butter or caramel chips.

Put into hot oven to melt the chips and brown the marshmallows. When marshmallows are puffy and golden brown, remove from the oven. Drizzle with syrups, top with sliced strawberries and serve with a scoop of ice cream.

MAKES 6 SERVINGS

**Pie dough for two
9-inch tarts***
2 cups walnuts
2 cups pecans
2 cups pistachios
2 cups almonds
1 cup pumpkin seeds
½ teaspoon salt
Bourbon Caramel Sauce

With Bourbon Caramel Sauce

*Use the Fail-Proof Pie Crust recipe on page 162. Or use pre-made frozen crusts if you are in a hurry.

Preheat oven to 350°F. Salt and roast nuts and seeds until golden brown, turning every few minutes to prevent burning, about 6 to 8 minutes. Set aside.

Roll out pie dough and put into two 9-inch tart pans. Cover dough with foil, making sure to cover the edges, and fill the foil-lined pans with uncooked rice or pie weights to keep the dough from puffing up.

Bake for 10 minutes. Remove pans from oven, remove rice and foil and return to oven to finish baking, 5 to 8 minutes more or until pie dough is light golden brown. Let cool while making the caramel sauce. When cooled, divide roasted nuts between the two tart shells. Pour caramel over both tarts (save remainder for serving) and bake until caramel bubbles, about 8 to 10 minutes. Let cool completely.

MAKES TWO 9-INCH TARTS

bourbon caramel sauce

2 cups sugar

⅓ cup water

½ teaspoon lemon juice

¾ cup honey

1½ cups Kentucky bourbon

2¾ cups whipping cream

3 tablespoons vanilla

3 tablespoons unsalted butter, softened

Combine sugar, water, lemon juice and honey in a large saucepan. Mix well. Cover and cook until sugar caramelizes and turns a medium golden brown. The best way is to cover the pan and let the steam clean the sugar off the sides.

Remove the pan from heat and whisk in the bourbon, then add the whipping cream and vanilla. Be careful; the sugar will bubble furiously and the bourbon will flame. Once the alcohol cooks off, it will no longer flame. Cook sugar mixture to 230°F (hard-ball stage). Remove from heat and whisk in softened butter.

MAKES 6 CUPS

key lime pie

CRUST

2 cups graham cracker crumbs

¾ cup melted butter

pinch salt

1 teaspoon sugar

1 teaspoon vanilla

FILLING

28 ounces sweetened condensed milk

1 cup Nellie and Joe's Key West Lime Juice
(see Resources)

5 egg yolks

1 lime, zested and juiced

TOPPING

1 pound cream cheese
(at room temperature)

1 lime, zested and juiced

2 tablespoons powdered sugar

Heat oven to 350°F. Mix together all ingredients for crust. Press into bottom and up sides of two 9-inch tart pans. Bake for 6 to 8 minutes and let cool.

FILLING

Mix together all ingredients and pour into graham-cracker crust. Bake at 350°F for 20 to 25 minutes. Do not overcook or filling will curdle. Cool on a rack and refrigerate. When pie is cold, spread on cream cheese topping. Serve with Margarita Key Lime Pie Sauce.

MAKES TWO 9-INCH PIES

TOPPING

Mix all ingredients and refrigerate until ready to use.

MARGARITA KEY LIME SAUCE

4 tablespoons cornstarch

1 cup powdered sugar

1 cup margarita mix

1 cup tequila or agave wine

1 lime, zested and juiced

Mix cornstarch and sugar in a small bowl. Put margarita mix, tequila or wine, and lime juice in a non-reactive saucepan and whisk in the cornstarch mixture. Boil for 2 minutes. Remove from heat and mix in zest and juice. Taste for sweetness and add more sugar. Let cool.

MAKES 3 CUPS

chocolate cream pie

With Chocolate Cookie Crust

CRUST

1⅓ cups chocolate wafer crumbs
(about 26 chocolate wafers)

5 tablespoons unsalted butter, melted

¼ cup sugar

FILLING

⅔ cup sugar

¼ cup cornstarch

½ teaspoon salt

1 tablespoon cocoa powder

4 large egg yolks

2 cups whole milk

1 cup heavy cream

7 ounces high-quality semisweet chocolate, melted

2 tablespoons unsalted butter, softened

1 teaspoon vanilla

TOPPING

¾ cup chilled whipping cream

1 tablespoon sugar

cocoa powder for dusting

Put oven rack in the middle position and heat oven to 350°F. Stir together crumbs, butter and sugar, and press into bottom and up sides of a 9-inch pie pan. Bake until crisp, about 15 minutes, and cool on a rack.

FILLING

Mix together sugar, cornstarch, salt and cocoa powder, then sift. Put yolks in a 3-quart heavy saucepan and add the sifted sugar mixture, mixing well.

Combine milk and cream and add to the mixture in the saucepan, slowly whisking the entire time. Bring to a boil over moderate heat, whisking, then reduce heat and simmer, whisking 1 minute more until filling is thick. If there are any lumps, strain the filling through a fine-mesh sieve into a bowl before adding the remaining ingredients.

Add chocolate, butter and vanilla to the filling and stir until chocolate melts. Pour filling into the pie crust and cover the surface with a buttered round of waxed paper. Chill in the refrigerator for 4-6 hours.

TOPPING

Whip cream and sugar until soft peaks form. Remove pie from the refrigerator, top with whipped cream and dust with cocoa powder.

MAKES ONE 9-INCH PIE

flourless chocolate cakes

2 cups semisweet chocolate, chopped

¾ pound butter, softened and divided in half

1 tablespoon vanilla

½ cup espresso
(or strong coffee)

½ cup merlot wine

1 cup sugar

1 cup cocoa powder

1 cup cornstarch

½ teaspoon baking powder

½ tablespoon xanthan gum
(see Resources)

pinch salt

3 eggs

1 cup semisweet chocolate chips
(or coarsely chopped bar)

sugar and cocoa powder for sprinkling

With Crème Anglaise

Best if made the day before serving. Preheat oven to 350°F. Melt the semisweet chocolate with half the butter, and mix in the vanilla, espresso and merlot. In a separate bowl, cream the rest of butter until fluffy. Add sugar and beat until light yellow and smooth about 5 minutes on high speed.

Mix together cocoa, cornstarch, baking powder, xanthan gum and salt. Add these dry ingredients and the chocolate mixture to butter and sugar, alternating, and mixing well after each addition. Add eggs one at a time, beating well after each egg, about 1 minute. Add semisweet chocolate chips. Pour into buttered cupcake tins or paper holders that have been sprinkled with sugar and cocoa powder.

Place a large open container of boiling water on the bottom rack of the oven. The steam helps cook the cakes and keeps them moist. Bake cakes on rack above the boiling water for 15 minutes. Turn off heat, open oven door and let rest for another 8 to 10 minutes. They should rise and be medium-soft to the touch. The trick here is to cook them long enough so they don't fall, but not so long that they are dry. Serve each cake in a puddle of Crème Anglaise, *(see page 176).*

Makes 16 individual cakes

5 egg yolks

¼ cup sugar

1 tablespoon cornstarch
(the French would not add cornstarch, but I do to thicken the sauce slightly)

pinch nutmeg

1½ cups milk

½ cup heavy cream

2 teaspoons vanilla extract

PASSION FRUIT CRÈME ANGLAISE

Follow recipe for Crème Anglaise and add

¼ cup Perfect Purée Passion Fruit Concentrate
(see Resources)

increase sugar to ⅓ cup

In a heat-resistant mixing bowl, stir together the egg yolks, sugar, cornstarch and nutmeg with a wooden spoon until well combined. The sugar should be somewhat dissolved in the yolks.

Combine the milk and cream in a medium saucepan over medium heat and warm the milk just below the boiling point (the milk will start to form bubbles on the edges of the pan and it will become steamy just before it boils).

Remove the pan from the heat and stir just a couple of tablespoons of the hot milk into the eggs and sugar, mixing well the whole time. Gradually add the rest of the milk, stirring constantly. Return the mixture to the saucepan over low to medium heat.

Heat the sauce until it thickens, but do not boil or the yolks will curdle. The sauce is done when it stays on the wooden spoon without dripping (this takes about five minutes but will depend on your pan and burner). As soon as the sauce is thickened, immediately remove it from the heat.

Pour the sauce into a heat-resistant bowl (you can pour the sauce through a strainer to remove any lumps).

Stir in the vanilla extract and cover the sauce with plastic wrap, pressing the wrap down on top of the sauce, and

new orleans bread pudding

With Southern Comfort Sauce

1 loaf day-old French bread

⅓ cup butter, melted

½ tablespoon cinnamon

¼ teaspoon ground cardamom

½ teaspoon nutmeg

½ teaspoon ground ginger

¾ cup granulated sugar, divided

½ cup apricot puree
(see Resources)

2 tablespoons vanilla

1 cup heavy cream

1 cup milk

2 eggs

½ cup golden raisins

1 cup apricots, diced

SAUCE

1 cup granulated sugar

1 tablespoon water

¼ teaspoon lemon juice

2 cups heavy cream

½ cup sour cream

1 cup Southern Comfort bourbon liqueur

1 tablespoon orange zest

2 tablespoons orange juice concentrate

Preheat oven to 350°F. Cut bread into cubes. Melt butter with cinnamon, cardamom, nutmeg, ginger and ¼ cup sugar and toss the bread cubes in this mixture. Put the bread cubes in the oven and toast until golden brown. Let cool.

Reduce oven temperature to 300°F. Mix together remaining ½ cup sugar, apricot puree, vanilla, heavy cream, milk and eggs.

Put toasted bread in a deep baking dish. Toss in raisins and apricots. Pour cream mixture over the bread. Cover with plastic wrap and weight it down with another baking dish or heavy plates, so that the bread is submerged and soaks up the liquid, for at least an hour.

Put the bread pudding in the oven and bake until it doesn't wiggle when moved, about 1 hour. Remove from oven and chill completely before cutting into squares. Serve with Southern Comfort Sauce.

MAKES 12 SERVINGS

SOUTHERN COMFORT SAUCE

Combine sugar, water and lemon juice in a saucepan. Cover and let boil until sugar caramelizes, about 15 minutes. When sugar is dark golden brown, add cream, sour cream and Southern Comfort. Cook to soft-ball stage on a candy thermometer. Remove from heat and stir in orange zest and orange juice concentrate.

MAKES 5 CUPS

carrot pumpkin cake

With Orange Cream Cheese Icing

1 cup walnuts,
toasted and chopped

1 cup coconut,
lightly toasted

LIQUID INGREDIENTS

1 cup carrots, grated

1 cup canned pumpkin

2 teaspoons lemon juice

4 eggs

¾ cup vegetable oil

1 cup crushed
pineapple, drained

DRY INGREDIENTS

1 tablespoon cinnamon

1 teaspoon each nutmeg,
allspice and ginger

1½ cups sugar

¾ cup brown sugar

1½ teaspoons baking soda

½ teaspoon baking powder

1 teaspoon salt

3 cups all-purpose flour

MILK MIXTURE

1 tablespoon vanilla

zest of 1 orange

1 cup milk

Preheat oven to 350°F. Toast walnuts and coconut for 10-12 minutes, tossing frequently. Put in a food processor and pulse until coarsely ground. Grease and flour three 9-inch cake pans. In a stand mixer, blend all the liquid ingredients. Mix all the dry ingredients in a separate bowl.

Mix vanilla and orange zest with milk. Alternate adding the dry ingredients and milk mixture to pumpkin/carrot mix. Blend well but do not overmix. Remove the bowl from the mixer and stir in the nuts and coconut.

Pour batter into greased, floured baking pans; smooth out the tops and put in the oven for 30-35 minutes. Cake is done when a toothpick inserted in the center comes out clean. Let cakes cool to room temperature, then refrigerate for at least 15 minutes before icing. While cakes are cooling, you can prepare the Orange Cream Cheese Icing.

MAKES ONE 3-LAYER CAKE

ICING

2 pounds cream cheese
(at room temperature)

1 orange, zested and juiced

3 tablespoons orange juice concentrate

½ cup powdered sugar

1 tablespoon vanilla

ORANGE CREAM CHEESE ICING

Whip cream cheese in a mixing bowl until soft and creamy. Add remaining ingredients and continue to mix for another minute or two. Frost cakes while the frosting is soft and both frosting and cakes are at room temperature.

MAKES 4 CUPS

TO ASSEMBLE CAKE

Before frosting, cut off the domed tops of each cake with a knife. This allows the layers to lay flat when frosted. It is easier to do this if the cake is slightly chilled.

Lay the first cake, cut side down, in the middle of a large cake plate and frost the top with Orange Cream Cheese Icing.

Position the second cake layer, cut side down, so it's even with the bottom layer, and frost the top. Add the third layer so it sits evenly on top of the bottom layers and frost the top and sides. Put cake in the freezer for 40 minutes.

Remove the cake from the freezer, slice, plate and let sit until the cake is nearly room temperature. Top each serving with vanilla ice cream or whipped cream.

berry crisp tart

TOPPING

1 cup oatmeal

1 cup all-purpose flour

½ cup brown sugar

2¼ teaspoons baking powder

1½ teaspoons cinnamon

¼ teaspoon salt

¼ pound butter, cut into small pieces

FILLING

5 cups mixed berries

2 lemons, zested and juiced

¾ cup granulated sugar

¼ cup cornstarch

1 tablespoon cinnamon

½ teaspoon nutmeg

CRUMBLE TOPPING

Put all dry ingredients into a food processor. Pulse lightly. Add chopped butter and pulse until dough is crumbly. Store, chilled, until ready to use.

FILLING

Preheat oven to 350°F. Pour lemon juice and zest over berries. Mix sugar, cornstarch, cinnamon and nutmeg. Sprinkle over berries and toss lightly. Taste berry mixture for sweetness; if too tart, add more sugar. Grease a 9x14-inch-deep baking pan. Pour in berry mixture and cover thoroughly with crumble topping. Press down lightly. Bake for about 40 minutes until bubbly and dark golden brown.

MAKES 8 TO 10 SERVINGS

banana macadamia

Tarte Tatin with Rum Caramel Sauce

All-purpose flour
(for work surface)

**2 sheets frozen
puff pastry, thawed**

**2 cups toasted, salted
macadamia nuts,
chopped**

Rum Caramel Sauce

**10 large ripe bananas,
peeled and halved
lengthwise**

Traditionally, tarte tatin is baked in a skillet, but you can use tart pans. Preheat oven to 400°F. Roll out one pastry sheet on a lightly floured work surface to a 13½-inch square. Using a large skillet as a guide, cut out a 12-inch round. Repeat with the second sheet of pastry.

Transfer pastry round to a baking sheet lined with parchment paper and chill until ready to use.

Have two 9-inch ovenproof skillets or tart pans ready. Sprinkle chopped macadamia nuts equally over both pans and cover with Rum Caramel Sauce. Arrange the bananas on top of the sauce, overlapping slightly as you layer. Place a pastry round on top of bananas and put in the oven. There will be an overhang, but puff pastry shrinks as it bakes.

Bake until pastry is golden brown and puffed, about 25 minutes. Remove from oven and let cool 10 minutes. Carefully invert each tart onto a serving plate. Serve warm or at room temperature. If refrigerated, cut slices and heat on individual plates in a 350°F oven for 6 minutes. Serve with Rum Caramel Sauce.

MAKES TWO 9-INCH TARTS

Rum Caramel Sauce

2 cups sugar
⅓ cup water
½ teaspoon lemon juice
¾ cup honey
2¾ cups whipping cream
1½ cups dark rum
3 tablespoons vanilla
3 tablespoons unsalted butter

Combine sugar, water, lemon juice and honey in a large saucepan. Mix well. Cover and cook until sugar caramelizes and turns a medium golden brown. The best way is to cover the pan and let the steam clean the sugar off the sides.

Remove the pan from the heat and whisk in the cream, rum, vanilla and butter. Be careful; the sugar will bubble furiously and the rum will flame. Once the alcohol cooks off, it will no longer flame. Cook sugar mixture to 230°F, hard-ball stage.

Makes 6 cups

The classic caramelized apple tarte tatin is right at the top of the list of traditional French desserts. Served upside down, it was the result of a happy accident that occurred at the Hotel Tatin, operated by two sisters in the early nineteenth century. Carolyn ran the business while Stephanie worked in the kitchen, and her apple tart was renowned for its caramel flavor and texture. During an especially busy time, Stephanie accidentally put the peeled apple quarters, butter and sugar directly in the pan, forgetting the pastry lining. Realizing her mistake, she added pastry to the top of the simmering apple mixture and put it back in the oven. When it was done she inverted the tarte, served it warm with crème fraîche, and a new dessert was born.

pecan tart

With Bourbon Caramel Sauce

Pie dough for two
9-inch tarts*

2 cups sugar

⅓ cup water

½ teaspoon lemon juice

¾ cup honey

2¾ cups whipping cream

1½ cups Kentucky bourbon

3 tablespoons vanilla

3 tablespoons unsalted
butter, softened

4 cups pecan halves,
lightly toasted and salted

*Use the Fail-Proof Pie Crust recipe
on page 162. Or use pre-made
frozen crusts if you are in a hurry.*

Heat oven to 350°F. Roll out pie dough and put into two springform pans. Cover dough with foil, making sure to cover the edges. Fill the foil-lined pans with uncooked rice or pie weights to keep the dough from puffing up. Bake for 10 minutes and remove pans from oven. Remove rice and foil and return pans to oven to finish baking, 5 to 8 minutes, or until pie dough is light golden brown. Remove shells from oven and let cool while making caramel sauce. Keep oven heated to 350°F.

Combine sugar, water, lemon juice and honey in a large saucepan. Mix well; cover and cook until sugar caramelizes and turns a medium golden brown, about 15 minutes. The best way to do this is to cover the pan and let the steam clean the sugar off the sides, removing the lid to check the color every 5 minutes.

When the sugar is a dark golden brown, remove the pan from the heat and whisk in the whipping cream, bourbon and vanilla. Be careful; the sugar will bubble furiously and the bourbon will flame. Once the alcohol cooks off, it will no longer flame. Cook sugar mixture to 230°F, hard-ball stage. Remove from heat and whisk in softened butter.

Divide toasted nuts between the two tart shells. Pour caramel sauce over both tarts (save remainder for serving) and bake at 350°F until caramel bubbles, about 8 to 10 minutes. Let cool completely.

MAKES TWO 9-INCH TARTS

mexican hot fudge sauce

½ **pound of high-quality fudge or fudge sauce**

1 **cup sweet red wine, like sangria**

½ **cup espresso or strong coffee**

1 **cup quality semisweet chocolate, chopped**

1 **cup heavy cream**

4 **tablespoons cinnamon**

¼ **cup garam masala**
(see Resources or page 198)

Combine all ingredients in a large double boiler and cook until mixture is soft and creamy. Serve with your favorite ice cream.

Makes 4 cups

handmade marshmallows

3 envelopes unflavored Knox gelatin

½ cup cold water

2 cups granulated sugar

⅔ cup corn syrup

¼ cup water

½ teaspoon salt

1 tablespoon vanilla extract

½ cup oil or spray

¼ cup cornstarch

¼ cup powdered sugar

SUGAR MIXTURE

2 cups granulated sugar

1½ cups light corn syrup

½ cup of water

¼ teaspoon of salt

In the bowl of a stand-up mixer, sprinkle gelatin over ½ cup cold water. Soak for 10 minutes.

Combine sugar, corn syrup, and ¼ cup water in a small saucepan. Bring to a boil and let boil for 1 minute. Pour boiling syrup into gelatin and mix at high speed. Add the salt and beat for 12 to 15 minutes more on high speed. Add vanilla and incorporate into mixture.

Lightly oil your hands, a spatula and a 9x12-inch baking pan with the oil or spray. Mix the cornstarch and powdered sugar together and sprinkle the oiled pan with half of this mixture; use a sifter or strainer. Spread marshmallow mixture evenly in the pan. Top the marshmallow mixture with the remaining cornstarch/powdered sugar mixture. Cover with plastic wrap or waxed paper and chill for 2 hours.

Remove from pan and cut into 10 rows long by 6 rows wide with scissors or a chef's knife.

Store at room temperature in an airtight container.

MAKES APPROXIMATELY 60 MARSHMALLOWS

butters & spices

taos garlic toast butter

1½ pounds butter
(at room temperature)

½ cup fresh garlic, chopped

½ cup fresh parsley, chopped

**1½ tablespoons
Spanish paprika**
(see Resources)

1½ tablespoons garlic powder

1½ tablespoons onion powder

1½ teaspoons black pepper

1½ teaspoons salt
(or to taste)

Combine all ingredients in a food processor or mixing bowl. Blend well. Store in a sealed container in the refrigerator. This butter makes the BEST garlic toast you have ever tasted. Also try it on grilled meats, vegetables, pasta and sandwiches.

MAKES 2 POUNDS

cilantro lime butter

1⅔ cups butter
(at room temperature)

1 lime, zested and juiced

**1 teaspoon New Mexican
red chili powder**
(see Resources)

⅔ teaspoon garlic powder

⅔ teaspoon kosher salt

2½ teaspoons cumin

1¾ teaspoons oregano

2¼ tablespoons cilantro

pinch pepper

pinch dried parsley

Put all ingredients into a food processor or mixing bowl and mix well. Cover and refrigerate until needed. Use this butter for both grilled and fried fish.

Makes 2 cups

macadamia nut butter

1 cup macadamia nuts, toasted

1 teaspoon sugar

2 teaspoons fresh cilantro, minced

½ teaspoon fresh thyme, minced

1 teaspoon lemon zest

coarse salt and fresh-ground pepper

1 pound butter, softened

Put all ingredients except butter into a food processor and pulse to a fine chop. Then work this mixture into the softened butter.

Roll butter mixture like a log in waxed paper and then wrap in plastic and store in the refrigerator. When ready to use, slice into ½ or 1-inch rounds. It pairs beautifully with fish like mahi mahi, ono, red snapper, shark and tuna.

MAKES 3 CUPS

garam masala butter

1 pound salted butter, softened

¼ cup orange zest

2 teaspoons garam masala
(see Resources or page 198)

½ teaspoon ground white pepper

pinch each cinnamon and nutmeg

Combine all ingredients in a stand mixer or food processor and mix until well blended. Roll the butter mixture like a log in parchment paper, wrap in plastic and store in the refrigerator. When ready to use, slice in ½ or 1-inch rounds.

This butter is beautiful on chicken, pork, halibut and scallops. You can also use it to spice up carrots, sweet potatoes and other vegetables. It is a delicious seasoning for couscous and rice or as a spread for herbed flatbread.

MAKES 2¼ CUPS

savory spice mix

1 cup New Mexican
red chile powder
(see Resources)

⅓ cup ground cumin

⅓ cup salt

2 tablespoons cinnamon

1 tablespoon black pepper

1 tablespoon dried
thyme leaves

2 cups dark brown sugar

Mix ingredients together and store in a cool dry place for up to 6 months. This mix is delicious on fall vegetables like sweet potatoes, pumpkin, squash and root vegetables. Try it on grilled lamb chops, steaks and chicken legs.

MAKES 4 CUPS

grilling spice

½ cup blue corn chips, ground

½ cup blue corn flour
(see Resources)

1 cup semolina

½ cup rice flour

¼ cup New Mexican
red chile powder
(see Resources)

1 tablespoon oregano

1 teaspoon cumin

1½ teaspoons garlic powder

1½ teaspoons onion powder

1 teaspoon salt

Mix all ingredients together and store in a cool dry place. I use this spice for local Taos trout, but it's perfect for any fried fish, and very good on chicken.

MAKES 2¾ CUPS

cajun spice blend

½ cup New Mexican
red chile powder
(see Resources)

¼ cup Spanish paprika
(see Resources)

¼ cup kosher salt

⅛ cup black pepper

2¼ teaspoons onion powder

2¼ teaspoons garlic powder

2¼ teaspoons dried oregano

pinch cayenne pepper

Mix and store in a cool dry place for up to 6 months. Excellent on chips, sweet potatoes and French fries made with Yukon gold potatoes. You can also add it to jambalaya, sautéed corn, fried oysters, fish stew and use it in traditional red beans and rice.

Once you start using this blend, you'll find it spices up just about everything. Be careful, it's addictive!

MAKES 1¼ CUPS

lamb spice crust

4 tablespoons plus 2 teaspoons
dark brown sugar

4 tablespoons plus 2 teaspoons
New Mexican red chile powder
(see Resources)

2 teaspoons ground cumin

2⅔ teaspoons garlic powder

3½ teaspoons salt

pinch dry mustard

pinch black pepper

pinch dried thyme leaves

Mix and store in a cool dry place. Use as a dry rub on lamb before roasting or grilling.

MAKES ⅔ CUP

garam masala

¼ cup coriander seeds

¼ cup cumin seeds

¼ cup black peppercorns

1 tablespoon whole cloves

1 tablespoon ground cinnamon

1 tablespoon green cardamom pods

Toast coriander and cumin seeds in a hot skillet, tossing to prevent burning, for 3-5 minutes. Combine with the other ingredients and grind in a blender or with a mortar and pestle. Store in a bottle or glass jar for up to 6 months.

MAKES 1 CUP

harissa

1 cup red pepper flakes

3 tablespoons
sweet paprika

3 cloves garlic, minced

1 teaspoon
ground coriander

3 teaspoons
ground caraway

2 teaspoons water

4-6 tablespoons olive oil

In a food processor or blender combine the pepper flakes, paprika, garlic, coriander, caraway, water and 4 tablespoons olive oil. Puree until mixture forms a paste, adding additional oil and/or water if necessary.

Transfer to a jar and cover with olive oil. Harissa will keep in the refrigerator for up to 6 months.

MAKES 1 CUP

mexican mole spice rub

¼ cup sesame seeds, toasted

⅓ cup cocoa powder

⅓ cup brown sugar

¼ cup salt

1 tablespoon each
New Mexican red chile powder
and Ancho chile powder
(see Resources)

1 tablespoon each
ground ginger,
ground cinnamon,
ground black pepper,
ground fennel
and ground oregano

Toast the sesame seeds in a hot skillet until fragrant and lightly browned, tossing frequently, for 3-5 minutes. Grind the toasted seeds with a mortar and pestle and mix with the rest of the ingredients until well blended. Store in an airtight container in a dry place for up to 6 months.

Use this rub on pork chops, chicken, turkey, duck breast, salmon and halibut. Add to 2 cups of New Mexican red chile sauce and 1 cup canned or fresh tomatilloes for a wonderful sauce. This spice mix has endless uses. Experiment; you will love it.

MAKES 1½ CUPS

NM green chile sauce

1 to 2 tablespoons
unsalted butter

1½ cups onion, chopped

2 large cloves garlic, minced

4 tablespoons browned flour
(see below)

3 cups chicken or
vegetable broth

2 cups green chile, chopped

½ teaspoon each ground
cumin and dried oregano

salt to taste

FLOUR

4 cups flour

Melt 1 tablespoon butter in a saucepan over medium heat. Add the onion and sauté until clear and soft, then add the garlic. Add more butter if needed. Stir in the browned flour and the broth and mix until smooth. Add chile, cumin and oregano and simmer for 10 to 15 minutes. Remove from heat and taste to adjust for salt and heat.

MAKES 4 CUPS

BROWNED FLOUR

Put a clean, dry skillet on the stove over high heat. When the pan is hot, add the flour and stir continually until the flour starts to brown and smell nutty. Be careful not to let it burn. Once the flour is golden brown, immediately remove the pan from the heat.

You will need this for any recipe that uses chile sauce. Make in advance and store, sealed, in the refrigerator.

NM red chile sauce

3 tablespoons butter

2 tablespoons browned flour
(see left)

¼ teaspoon each ground cumin and dried oregano

½ cup New Mexican red chile powder
(see Resources)

1 cup cold water

2 to 3 cups chicken or vegetable broth

1 clove garlic, minced

salt to taste

Melt butter in a saucepan over medium heat. Add the onion and sauté until clear and soft, then add the garlic. Add the browned flour and stir until smooth. Next, add the cumin and oregano and remove the pan from the heat.

Mix the ground chile with cold water until there are no lumps. Whisk it into the flour paste in the saucepan. Return to the heat and slowly whisk in the broth. Simmer for 20 minutes, stirring frequently. If the sauce is lumpy, pulse it in the blender for a few seconds.

MAKES 4 CUPS

peach BBQ sauce

1 cup peach nectar

¼ cup dried peaches

3 tablespoons ketchup

1 teaspoon chipotle
in adobo sauce

3 tablespoons
red wine vinegar

2 tablespoons olive oil

1½ teaspoons dried rosemary

1½ teaspoons dried oregano

1½ teaspoons liquid smoke

salt to taste

Combine peach nectar and dried peaches in a small saucepan. Bring to a boil and turn off heat. Cover and let sit to cool. Once cooled, put in blender and mix until dried peaches are smooth. Add remaining items to blender and mix until sauce is smooth.

MAKES 2 CUPS

pineapple salsa

2 cups pineapple, diced

1 red bell pepper,
seeded and diced

1 clove garlic, minced

2 limes, zested and juiced

2 jalapeños, seeded and diced

¼ cup sugar

2 tablespoons cilantro, minced

½ teaspoon salt

¼ teaspoon
Cholula hot sauce
(see Resources)

Mix all ingredients together and refrigerate until ready to use. This salsa will keep for 2 weeks. Use on quesadillas, grilled shrimp, chicken breasts; just about all seafood and poultry. Pour it over cream cheese for an instant dip. Serve it as a side dish for enchiladas and fish tacos.

MAKES 2½ CUPS

cilantro pesto

2 cups cilantro, packed tight

½ cup almonds, blanched

¼ cup red onion, chopped

½ teaspoon serrano chile, seeded and chopped

½ teaspoon kosher salt

¼ cup olive oil

In a food processor, pulse the cilantro, almonds, onion, chile, and salt until well blended. With the food processor running, add the olive oil in a slow, steady stream.

This pesto will keep in the refrigerator for 3 days or frozen for later use. Toss with pasta and Cotija cheese. Make a chorizo and tomato pizza with Cilantro Pesto and Monterey Jack cheese. Use it on grilled chicken or in tomato sandwiches. Mix and use as a dressing for bean or rice salads. If you love the taste of cilantro like I do, you will use it for just about anything.

MAKES 2 CUPS

prickly pear margarita sauce

¼ cup sugar

2 tablespoons cornstarch

1 cup agave wine
or tequila

2 cups prickly pear, thawed
(see Resources)

1 lime, zested and juiced

salt to taste

Combine the sugar and cornstarch and add the wine or tequila, stirring well. Put in a saucepan with all other ingredients and bring to a boil. Remove from heat and taste for hotness. If a spicier sauce is wanted, add a good quality Mexican hot sauce to taste. Delicious with grilled chicken breast.

MAKES 3 CUPS

green chile hollandaise

8 egg yolks

1 pound butter, melted

4 tablespoons
lemon juice

½ teaspoon salt

pinch New Mexican
green chile powder
(see Resources)

pinch cornstarch or guar gum
(see Resources)

½ cup green chile, drained,
chopped and heated

Separate eggs, saving yolks. Melt the butter in a saucepan or microwave. Put eggs yolks in a blender and add lemon juice, salt, cornstarch and chile powder. Mix at high speed, then reduce to medium speed and slowly add melted butter until the yolks start to thicken. Don't rush this stage. Taste to adjust seasonings.

Put hollandaise sauce into a bowl, adding the warm chopped chile and serve immediately. If hollandaise sauce sets too long it will get cold; if it's too hot, it will separate.

For traditional hollandaise sauce, omit the green chile and green chile powder. It's just as good; in fact I made my reputation on Eggs Benedict with Hollandaise at our restaurant in Sonoma, California. We would go through 3 soup kettles of hollandaise sauce on Sunday mornings; that's about 33 quarts or 1,056 ounces!

MAKES 10 TO 12 SERVINGS

apricot chipotle sauce

½ cup brown sugar

½ cup plus 2 tablespoons cornstarch

2 tablespoons cumin

1 tablespoon garam masala
(see Resources or page 198)

1 teaspoon oregano

2 cups apricot puree
(see Resources)

1 cup sherry wine

½ cup fresh lime juice

½ to 1 whole 7-ounce can chipotle in adobo sauce

2 tablespoons chicken base
(see Resources)

Mix sugar and cornstarch together and add dry spices. Mix wet ingredients, and add dry mixture until well blended. Cook in a saucepan, stirring constantly until sauce comes to boil. Taste for heat and sweetness and adjust to taste. Delicious with pork or chicken.

MAKES 4 CUPS

ras el hanout

4 teaspoons cumin seed

4 teaspoons ground ginger

5 teaspoons coriander seeds

2 tablespoons
black peppercorns

2 tablespoons
ground cinnamon

1 teaspoon
cayenne pepper

16 whole cloves

20 allspice berries

This popular blend of herbs and spices is used throughout North Africa, especially in Morocco. The name means "head of the shop" in Moroccan Arabic, and refers to a mixture of the best spices a seller has to offer. This is my personal recipe.

Grind all ingredients together in a blender or with a mortar and pestle. Store in an airtight jar and it will keep for 6 months.

MAKES 1 CUP

lesley's black bean spice

¼ cup ground fennel

¼ cup ground cumin

¼ cup New Mexican
chile powder
(see Resources)

1 tablespoon dried oregano

½ tablespoon garlic powder

½ tablespoon onion powder

1 teaspoon sugar

1½ tablespoons salt

Mix all ingredients together and store in a cool dry place. I use this spice mix primarily to season black beans, but it's also great on veggies and meats.

MAKES 1 CUP

lesley's frijoles negros

2 (15-ounce) cans black beans

3 tablespoons Lesley's Black Bean Spice
(see left)

1 tablespoon masa harina or cornmeal

Mix all ingredients together in a cold saucepan. Heat until the beans start to bubble around the edges and the sauce thickens. Stir frequently to prevent the beans from burning.

MAKES 6 SERVINGS

resources, shortcuts and tips

RESODRCES

COOK'S THESAURUS
An online cooking encyclopedia, *www.foodsubs.com,* covers thousands of ingredients. Entries have pictures, description, synonyms, pronunciations and suggested substitutions. I love this website!

BASES
Beef, chicken, fish, seafood (including crab, shrimp and lobster) bases are available from Better Than Bouillon online at *www.superiortouch.com* or from Minor's at *www.wholey.com.* They are also sold at Costco, Wal-Mart, Kroger's and Whole Foods, although not every store carries all varieties. If you cannot find seafood base, substitute crab or shrimp base.

CREAM OF COCONUT
Coco Lopez cream of coconut can be found in any liquor store.

FLOURS AND GRAINS
Blue corn and semolina can be found at *www.bobsredmill.com* or in most health food stores and high-end grocers.
Rice flour — *www.bobsredmill.com.*

Risotto rice — risotto is made with Arborio rice, which when cooked, is called risotto. It is available in most supermarkets or from *www.bobsredmill.com.*

FRUIT AND FRUIT PUREES
Any kind of fruit puree can be found at *www.perfectpuree.com.* Perfect Purees are available at some Whole Foods stores and Central Markets in Texas.

Meyer lemon concentrate — *www.perfectpuree.com.*

Nielsen's Citrus lemon concentrate — *www.nielsenscitrus.com.*

Preserved lemons — *www.igourmet.com.*

FRUIT JUICES AND NECTARS
www.jumex.com.

GLUTEN FREE
Breads — Udi's gluten free burger buns and other gluten free breads — *www.udisglutenfree.com.*

Grains — rice flour, chickpea flour and nut flours — *www.bobsredmill.com.*

Polenta — Ancient Harvest Quinoa. *www.foodservicedirect.com.*

GUMS

Xanthan or guar — *www.bobsredmill.com*. Gums create viscosity when added to foods that do not contain gluten stabilizers.

KEY LIME JUICE

Nellie and Joe's Key West Lime Juice is available from *www.keylimejuice.com* or *www.amazon.com*.

MEXICAN CHEESES

Look in the cheese section of your supermarket or any Mexican grocery.

NORI

Japanese seaweed is available from *www.amazon.com* or *www.mothernature.com*.

OILS

Brazilian dendê oil can be bought online at *www.amigofoods.com*.

Moroccan argan oil is available from *www.amazon.com*.

PASTA SHEETS

Fresh pasta sheets are available from *www.epicurious.com* or *www.amazon.com*.

POMEGRANATE MOLASSES

www.americanspice.com.

SAUCES

Pickapeppa Sauce — *www.cajungrocer.com*.

Nam Pla Thai Fish Sauce — available in the Asian section of most supermarkets.

Hoisin Sauce — available in the Asian section of most supermarkets.

Huyfong Sriracha Sauce — also called Rooster sauce *www.huyfong.com*.

Mae Ploy Sweet Thai Chili Sauce — *www.importfood.com*.

SPICES AND CHILES OR CHILIS

Annatto seeds — *www.myspicesage.com*.

Asian — *www.myspicesage.com*.

   Chinese five-spice powder

   Star anise

   Tuxedo sesame seeds

Cajun or Creole — *www.cajungrocer.com*.

Indian — *www.myspicesage.com*.

   Garam masala

   Indian red curry

Jamaican — *www.myspicesage.com*.
Jamaican jerk seasoning

Mexican and New Mexican —
www.chileguy.com.

   Ancho chile powder

   Chimayo Chile

   Chipotle in adobo sauce —
   in the Mexican section of
   most supermarkets.

   Cumin

   Guajillo Chile

   Mexican oregano

   New Mexican chile sauces
   and powders

Middle Eastern — *www.worldspice.com*
and my favorite, *www.zamourispices.com.*

   Ras el Hanout
   (also spelled Ras el Hanouf)

   Harissa

Mexican — *www.mexgrocer.com.*

   Achiote paste

New Mexican Spice mixes —
www.santafeseasons.com.

Spanish — *www.spanishtable.com.*

   Spanish paprika

Sumac — *www.myspicesage.com.*

Turkish — *www.myspicesage.com* or
www.worldspice.com.

   Turkish red pepper paste

TAMALES
Many kinds of tamales are available at
your local supermarket. They can also
be found at Trader Joe's, Whole Foods
and your local Mexican Restaurant.
Online sources are:
www.santafetamales.com or
www.cornmaiden.com.

SHORTCUTS

I am a firm believer in "keep it simple"
and I use pre-made ingredients whenever needed. After all, big companies
spend millions of dollars on product
development to insure that ready-
made products turn out perfect every
time. Don't shy away from store-
bought items when cooking; after
all who really has time to make puff
pastry from scratch? Here are some
items that have my blessing. They are
all highly rated and will save you time
and stress.

Frozen Pie Crust
Two brands that stand out above the rest are Wholly Wholesome Organic and Pillsbury Pet-Ritz. Both are carried in most supermarket frozen-food sections.

Puff Pastry Sheets
Pepperidge Farm — usually the only brand carried by most supermarkets, and it is a great product.

Biscuit Mix
Bisquick, King Arthur, Krusteaz or Pioneer are all good brands. You can turn out a quick coffee cake, banana bread, pancakes or just flaky biscuits without breaking a sweat.

Cake Mixes
For white cakes add any of the following: vanilla extract, almond extract, coconut extract, orange juice concentrate, orange or lemon zest. You can also substitute coconut milk for water.

For chocolate cakes, add: vanilla extract, almond extract or cherry extract. Substitute coffee for water and add cocoa powder.

Ice Cream
You can make a special dessert by adding flavor to vanilla ice cream. Try toasted nuts, chocolate pieces, orange concentrate or liqueurs. Let the ice cream soften slightly, put it in a stand-up mixer and add your ingredients. Refreeze in a covered baking dish for about an hour.

Green Chiles
Canned green chile can be found in the Mexican section of your super-market. Green chile is also available in the frozen-food section or from your local Mexican grocery. Whether canned or frozen, it is always roasted and the heat of the chile is specified on the package or can.

Roasted Red Peppers
Mezzetta offers good quality, but there are many others available, packed in water or oil; I prefer packed in water so they aren't oily when handled.

Red and Green Chile Sauce
Check the Mexican section at your local supermarket or any Mexican grocery. If you cannot find chile sauce, use red or green enchilada sauce and add ½ teaspoon each dried oregano and powdered cumin per can.

Black Beans
Canned or low-sodium black beans are a great substitute for the time-consuming task of cooking your own beans.

Blue Corn Chips
Buy a bag of your favorite chips, and before serving, heat them in the microwave for a few seconds. When warmed they taste home made.

Salsa
Use your favorite brand and doctor it with some chopped green chile, cumin and fresh cilantro.

Vinaigrette
Have at least 2 bottles of your favorite on hand for those times when you are up against the clock and you want to make the Cranberry Vinaigrette.

Frozen Berries
Use frozen blueberries, blackberries, strawberries and raspberries to make crisps, galettes and tarts. A bag of berries and your frozen pie or puff pastry dough will save you when you need a great dessert fast.

Frozen Tamales
There are many good brands available. Try Trader Joe's and Whole Foods.

Lime and Lemon Juice
This is where I really balk, since there is nothing like fresh juices; but if you are in a pinch, Sicilia is the best brand. Another tip is to squeeze lots of lemons and limes and freeze the juice in an ice cube tray to use whenever you need.

TIPS

HOW TO CARAMELIZE ONIONS
Caramelizing onions means cooking them down until the sugars within the onion turn to caramel. It's easy to do, and they are absolutely delicious. Even onions that smell strong will become sweet and tender after caramelizing.

2 yellow onions
2 tablespoons canola oil

Peel and slice the onions. It's important to have all the onion slices uniform so they cook evenly. Heat a large non-stick frying pan over medium heat. Add the oil and continue to heat until the oil is hot but not smoking; add the onions. The onions should sizzle. Stir them well so each slice gets coated with the oil.

Let the onions cook, stirring them up from the bottom frequently, so they cook evenly. *Do not cover. Continue stirring from time to time, bringing the browned onions on the bottom up to the top.*

The onions will start to lose their water and then begin to brown. Once browning starts, lower the heat so the onions don't burn. From this point, you need to watch them closely and stir more frequently. As the sugar begins to caramelize, the onions will turn from light tan to golden to brown. When the desired color is reached (about 15 to 25 minutes), remove the onions from the pan to cool.

HOW TO PREPARE FRESH TOMATILLOES

Put tomatilloes, with their husks, in a bowl and cover with hot tap water. Let them soak for a few minutes. One at a time, peel off the husks and remove the stem with a paring knife. You can chop them raw for fresh salsa or cut them in half and simmer for 8-10 minutes for cooked salsas and other recipes.

HOW TO MAKE A FRUIT PUREE

Wonderful fruit purees and concentrates can be bought online from *www.perfectpuree.com*, but if you want to make your own, try this recipe for a basic fruit puree. *Jumex Juices* can be found in your supermarket, Mexican grocery or online at *www.mexgrocer.com*.

2 cups fruit nectar or Jumex Juice

8 ounces dried fruit

sugar to taste
(this will depend on the sweetness of the nectar or juice)

pinch of salt to enhance the fruit flavor

lemon or lime juice
(if the fruit juice is too sweet)

Stir all ingredients in a heavy saucepan over medium heat until the mixture simmers; then cover and continue cooking until the dried fruit softens, about 15 minutes. Cool and transfer mixture to a food processor and puree until smooth. Taste and adjust for salt, sugar, lemon or lime juice. Refrigerate until ready to use. Puree will keep for 1 week or indefinitely if frozen. I freeze purees in an ice cube tray and transfer the cubes to a plastic freezer bag for storage.

Purees can be made with either fresh fruit or frozen fruit and nectar. Here are some fresh fruit equivalents:

Mango — the pulp from 1 large or 2 small mangoes will yield 1 cup of puree.

Pineapple Guava — the pulp from 12 to 14 pineapple guavas will yield 1 cup of puree. If you cannot find pineapple guavas, use regular guavas or an equal combination of kiwi, pineapple and strawberry.

Lychee Fruit — the pulp from 12 to 14 lychee fruits will yield 1 cup of puree. If you cannot find lychee fruit use rambutans, longans or grapes.

Prickly Pear — the pulp from 1 large or 2 small prickly pears will yield 1 cup of puree. If you cannot find prickly pear, use pepino melon or as a last resort, watermelon.

Passion Fruit — the pulp from 12 passion fruits will yield 1 cup of puree. If you cannot find passion fruit, you can substitute guava or pineapple with some fresh lime.

How To Whip Egg Whites

Here are a few easy but important tips to perfectly whipped egg whites:

The bowl and beaters should be absolutely clean and dry.

When separating the eggs, you cannot have even one tiny little piece of egg yolk in the whites or they will not beat. Egg whites are sensitive to oil, yolk or water.

Egg whites like to be at room temperature. The proteins in the whites expand better when warm, so you will get more volume from the eggs.

Add a pinch of salt to the eggs before you begin, to help firm up the proteins.

Halfway through the beating process, add an acid (stabilizer) to the foam. I use cream of tartar, but one or two drops of lemon juice or vinegar will work as well.

chile

Straight From the Heart is a culinary journey. Read this section to learn some basic information about an ingredient found in many of the recipes: New Mexican red and green chile.

Green chile and red chile, in most cases, are actually the same plant, harvested at different times. Green chile season is late July through the end of September. Chile not harvested then is left in the field to turn red and comes to market in late fall, before the frost begins. Green chile is mainly roasted, and red chile is dried and ground into a powdered spice or hung for decoration in our traditional ristras.

In other parts of the country, you can find similar chile peppers called Anaheim and chile del norte, the dried red Anaheim.

When you see green chile in a recipe, it's always roasted. The heat in the chile comes from the seeds and veins. If you do not like it hot, be sure to remove all the seeds and veins.

Roasting fresh chile is simple:
You will need disposable gloves before you begin. When you roast chile over high heat, the skins blacken and blister. Peel off the skin and you'll find a treasure: sweet, tender flesh with a pleasantly smoky taste. Chiles are best roasted over a live fire, such a charcoal or gas grill. You can also use the burner on your gas range:

Turn the heat to high.

Using tongs, place the flesh of the chile directly in the flame of the burner or as close to the heat source as possible. Rotate the chile as the flesh closest to the heat blackens and blisters.

Remove the chile with tongs when it has blackened completely.

Put the blackened chile in a bowl, cover with plastic wrap and allow it to steam (or put it in a bag and seal it). Let them rest for 15 to 20 minutes.

Now put on the disposable gloves. While peeling and deveining the chile, do not touch your face, especially your eyes and lips. I have learned this the hard way. If you are working with extremely hot chile, wear glasses.

Remove chile from the bag; peel off and discard the blackened skin. Then slice open and remove the seeds, stem and inner ribs. If you like it hot, leave some of the seeds and ribs intact. At this time you can either use the chile or refrigerate it for up to one week.

Roasted chile also freezes well. If you want to freeze the chiles, lay them on a cookie sheet to freeze individually and, when frozen, store in freezer bags.

If you don't have a grill or gas burner, you can always use the oven broiler. Cut the chile in half and lay it cut side down. Oil it and place under the broiler for 5 to 7 minutes, turning with a pair of tongs.

Roasted green chile is available in the Mexican or frozen-food section of your local supermarket. It is packaged canned or frozen, whole or chopped.

The heat of the chile will be described as hot, medium, mild or illustrated by a little gauge on the can. If you live in New Mexico, Texas, Arizona or California, New Mexican chile, canned or frozen, is easy to find; otherwise use Anaheim.

Be sure and check out the **Resources, Shortcuts and Tips** section which lists online sources for hard-to-find ingredients and timesaving substitutions.

I invite you to join me on this culinary journey. Make *Straight from the Heart* your own cookbook; try the recipes and feel free to change them to suit your taste. Cooking is so much more than preparing a recipe by following the instructions — it's about engaging your creativity and excitement. Cooking is unique to each of us; it is an expression of love, straight from the heart.